Divine
Mercy
Minutes

Divine Mercy Minutes

Daily Gems of St. Faustina to Transform Your Prayer Life

Revised Edition

Arranged and Introduced by
Rev. George W. Kosicki, CSB

MARIAN PRESS
STOCKBRIDGE · MA 01263

2015

Available from:
Marian Helpers Center
Stockbridge, MA 01263

Prayerline:1-800-804-3823
Orderline: 1-800-462-7426
Website:www.marian.org

Imprimi Potest:
Very Rev. Walter M. Dziordz, MIC, D Min
Provincial Superior
November 27, 2005

Library of Congress Catalog Number: 2005935789

ISBN: 978-1-59614-200-8

Editing and Proofreading: David Came

Cover and Page Design: Catherine M. LeVesque

Cover and interior image: Skip Dean, www.skipdean.com

For texts from the English Edition of *Diary of St. Maria Faustina Kowalska*

Nihil Obstat:
George H. Pearce, SM
Former Archbishop of Suva, Fiji

Imprimatur:
Joseph F. Maguire
Bishop of Springfield, MA
April 9, 1984

Printed in the United States of America

Dedication

To His Holiness, now Pope Emeritus Benedict XVI, who continued the challenging and prophetic words of St. Pope John Paul II on Divine Mercy with "a mandate: go forth and be witnesses of God's mercy, a source of hope for every person and for the whole world" (*Regina Caeli* Message at the conclusion of the World Apostolic Congress on Mercy, St. Peter's Square, April 6, 2008).

Foreword

In the Summer of 2007, I had the opportunity to film segments of *Divine Mercy Minutes*, which are now seen on the Eternal Word Television Network (EWTN). The setting for the filming was ideal, since it was on the grounds of the beautiful National Shrine of The Divine Mercy in Stockbridge, Massachusetts, which is administered by the Marians of the Immaculate Conception.

I find it easy to pray at the National Shrine, because God seems to be so close to all the pilgrims who visit there. Our grounds are called Eden Hill, and it truly seems to be a place where heaven and earth meet.

I had previously done an audio recording of some *Divine Mercy Minutes* for broadcast on the radio, but in that recording session, I had only read passages from the *Diary of Saint Maria Faustina Kowalska*. Producing the video of *Divine Mercy Minutes* gave me the opportunity to meditate on the various passages from the *Diary* in order to give my own personal reflections.

That summer, I came to appreciate the simple and beautiful spirituality of St. Faustina in a new way. Despite her very limited education, it is obvious that the Holy Spirit guided her profoundly as she wrote her *Diary*. Some hope that she will some day be declared a Doctor of the Church. I find the *Diary* to be a treasure trove of wisdom for those who hope to grow in the spiritual life. Saint Faustina experienced great joys as well as profound trials, which she then wrote about in the notebooks that now comprise the *Diary*. We can't all identify with the extraordinary revelations that she received, but we can identify with her struggles.

The value of *Divine Mercy Minutes* is that it only takes a minute or two to read the two or three passages provided for each day, but they can provide spiritual nourishment for us that can last the whole day long. Like our Holy Mother Mary, we can ponder these things and reflect on them in our hearts. These spiritual morsels of mercy can inspire us to grow in a particular virtue or to avoid a particular vice. They can remind us that the Lord is merciful, that He cares for us, and that He has not forgotten us.

In the midst of our busy world, these *Divine Mercy Minutes* can become mini-meditations on the spiritual life. They can provide a structure for us to slow down for a minute, to turn our attention toward heaven, and get some perspective on what really matters. The Scriptures teach us that we must put on Christ and view the world with the eyes of faith. The writings of St. Faustina can help to give us that heavenly perspective.

May you be blessed through your use of this book. Don't rush through it! Read it prayerfully every day with the help of the Holy Spirit. As you do, I am convinced that you will gain as much as I did from it. God bless you!

Fr. Joseph G. Roesch, MIC
General Promoter of Eucharistic Apostles of The Divine Mercy

Introduction

> O Holy Trinity, Eternal God, I want
> to shine in the crown of Your mercy
> as a tiny gem whose beauty depends
> on the ray of Your light and of Your
> inscrutable mercy (*Diary of St. Faustina*,
> 617).

This collection of inspirational statements from the
Diary are like *gems* that glisten with the radiance of
God's mercy. These gems are in St. Faustina's own
words, but the Lord gave her "an interior light by
which I learned that not a single word was mine;
despite difficulties and adversities, I have always,
always, fulfilled His will, as He made it known to
me" (*Diary*, 1667). So, according to her words,
these gems are what the Lord wanted recorded in
her *Diary*, all for our benefit. (See *Diary*, 895, 1142,
1317, 1471.)

This mining of gems of St. Faustina is a companion
and a complement to the booklet *Come to My Mercy:
The Desires and Promises of the Merciful Savior as
recorded in the Diary of St. Faustina* (Marian Press,
DML12). *Come to My Mercy* is really a collection of
the *gems of Jesus*, gathering together the words of the
Lord on The Divine Mercy message and devotion,
while this present companion devotional gathers the
best of the many gems that St. Faustina records in

response to the words of the Lord about Divine Mercy message and devotion. Saint Faustina really wanted to be a "tiny gem" in the crown of mercy that the Lord wears, with all its beauty and sparkle coming from His mercy. She wanted to be a living jewel, a crystal radiating the Lord's light. She wanted to be a saint:

> I am going to strive for the greatest purity of soul, that the rays of God's grace may be reflected in all their brilliance. I long to be a crystal in order to find favor in His eyes (*Diary*, 805).

Saint Faustina knew where to go to gather the precious jewels of God's grace. She knew the source of all graces and mercy — the pierced, merciful Heart of Jesus. She knew how to gather them:

> Today I saw the Crucified Lord Jesus. Precious pearls and diamonds were pouring forth from the wound in His Heart. I saw how a multitude of souls was gathering these gifts, but there was one soul who was closest to His Heart and she, knowing the greatness of these gifts, was gathering them with liberality, not only for herself, but for others as well. The Savior said to me,

Behold, the treasures of grace that flow down upon souls, but not all souls know how to take advantage of My generosity (*Diary* 1687).

The Lord taught St. Faustina how to gather the graces flowing from His pierced Heart, namely, by gazing upon His merciful Heart in contemplation:

Today, the Lord said to me, My daughter, look into My Merciful Heart and reflect its compassion in your own heart and in your deeds, so that you, who proclaim My mercy to the world, may yourself be aflame with it (*Diary*, 1688).

These gems of St. Faustina are intended as an aid to the growth of your spiritual life. They can be "maxims for the day" — reflected upon over and over during the day. They are instructive and inspirational. Through them, your daily prayer can become "Divine Mercy Minutes." Use them for your benefit as the Lord told St. Faustina:

My daughter, you do not live for yourself but for souls; write for their benefit (*Diary*, 895).

My daughter, be diligent in writing down every sentence I tell you concerning My mercy, because this is meant for a great number of souls who will profit from it (*Diary*, 1142).

This selection of the gems of St. Faustina originated from the summary of each paragraph entry of her *Diary* under ninety topics in my preparation of the *Thematic Concordance to the Diary of Saint Maria Faustina Kowalska* (Marian Press, **SGD2**). One of the topics was "Gems of Sr. Faustina." Over the years more gems were added and then printed out on the computer. The best of the gems were selected and then categorized under major topics.

Jason Free — a good friend — and I read though the gems and marked those that struck us as extra special. They are marked with a cross †. Mark your own gems. Make your own collection of "pearls and diamonds."

Each new topic is introduced by a reflection to help you appreciate the gems that follow for your daily "Divine Mercy Minutes."

Some special notes to the reader: The references to the *Diary* are noted as (*Diary* _ _). The number refers to the paragraphs in the *Diary*. Also, gems are frequently repeated under different themes. When this is the case, the reader is invited to consider a different facet of the gem under the new theme. Examine the gem from a different angle and discover afresh its beauty. Seek to deepen your understanding of the spiritual truth being considered. (An index of all the themes is included at the back of this book.)

The dove of the Holy Spirit is used as a design motif to recall the special devotion of St. Faustina to the Holy Spirit. As she recorded, "Faithfulness to the inspirations of the Holy Spirit — that is the shortest route [to holiness]" (*Diary*, 291). For more of her gems on the Holy Spirit, see the entries for December 12-14.

Further, this devotional follows the convention of the *Diary* for boldface and italics. That is, the words of Jesus are in boldface, while the words of Mary are in italics.

Special thanks to Christine Kruszyna, my secretary, who finalized the text of the *Diary* onto the computer from the scanning done by Mike Sherry. She then "cut and pasted" by computer the gems into the present categories. And to Janice Devlin a blessing of Divine Mercy for typing *Divine Mercy Minutes* in this daily format.

Extra special thanks to David Came, executive editor of Marian Press, for his dedicated work on the manuscript and especially for the addition of the titles for the daily entries, which throw light on the gems and made them sparkle! Also, congratulations to Catherine M. LeVesque, the book designer, for her marvelous design of the cover and the pages using the magnificent dove motif.

May you be inspired by the Holy Spirit as you read and reflect on these gems of St. Faustina each day. May they become a treasure chest of graces for you.

Fr. George W. Kosicki, CSB

Trust

January 1 - 17

The key to St. Faustina's spiritual life was trust in Jesus. It is expressed in the inscription of every Divine Mercy Image: *"Jesus, I trust in You!"* This trust in Jesus is a combination of faith, hope, and love. Trust is *hope*, which is a reliance on the promises of Jesus, based on *faith or belief* in Jesus and expressed in *love* for God and neighbor. Pope John Paul II describes trust in the words of St. Elizabeth to the Blessed Virgin Mary: "Blessed are you for trusting that the word of God would be fulfilled in you." John Paul II, writes "To believe/to trust/means to abandon oneself to the truth of the word of the living God" (*Mother of the Redeemer*, 1987).

Put into a mnemonic, it is:
TRUST =" **T**otal **R**eliance **U**pon **S**aving **T**ruth," which is Jesus Christ.

The following gems of St. Faustina on *trust* challenge us to "trust in Jesus *even more!*"

I Fear Nothing

O my Jesus, despite the deep night that is all around me and the dark clouds which hide the horizon, I know that the sun never goes out. O Lord, though I cannot comprehend You and do not understand Your ways, I nonetheless trust in Your mercy (*Diary*, 73).

Oh, I fear nothing; if God sends such great suffering to a soul, He upholds it with an even greater grace, although we are not aware of it. One act of trust at such moments gives greater glory to God than whole hours passed in prayer filled with consolations. Now I see that if God wants to keep a soul in darkness, no book, no confessor can bring it light (*Diary*, 78).

Guide Me

† With the trust and simplicity of a small child,
I give myself to You today, O Lord Jesus, my
Master. I leave You complete freedom in directing
my soul. Guide me along the paths You wish.
I won't question them. I will follow You trustingly.
Your merciful Heart can do all things! (*Diary*, 228).

Today I place my heart on the paten where Your
Heart has been placed, O Jesus, and today I offer
myself together with You to God, Your Father
and mine, as a sacrifice of love and praise. Father
of Mercy, look upon the sacrifice of my heart,
but through the wound in the Heart of Jesus
(*Diary*, 239).

*H*E IS LORD

God is my Father and so I, His child, have every claim to His divine Heart; and the greater the darkness, the more complete our trust should be (*Diary*, 357).

† I do not understand how it is possible not to trust in Him who can do all things. With Him, everything; without Him, nothing. He is Lord. He will not allow those who have placed all their trust in Him to be put to shame (*Diary*, 358).

ONE TRUSTED FRIEND

† Often have I lived hoping against hope, and have advanced my hope to complete trust in God. Let that which He has ordained from all ages happen to me (*Diary*, 386).

I have only one trusted Friend in whom I confide everything, and that is Jesus — the Eucharist, and His representative — my confessor (*Diary*, 504).

O Father Of Mercy

All my nothingness is drowned in the sea of Your mercy. With the confidence of a child, I throw myself into Your arms, O Father of Mercy, to make up for the unbelief of so many souls who are afraid to trust in You (*Diary*, 505).

I have placed my trust in God and fear nothing. I have given myself over to His holy will; let Him do with me as He wishes, and I will still love Him (*Diary*, 589).

Distrust Hurts His Most Sweet Heart

God is very displeased with lack of trust in Him, and this is why some souls lose many graces. Distrust hurts His most sweet Heart, which is full of goodness and incomprehensible love for us (*Diary*, 595).

When the burden of the battle becomes too much for me, I throw myself like a child into the arms of the heavenly Father and trust I will not perish (*Diary*, 606).

My Strength And My Only Hope

I trust in You, O merciful God, and I wish to be the first to manifest to You that confidence which You demand of souls (*Diary*, 615).

My Jesus, my strength and my only hope, in You alone is all my hope. My trust will not be frustrated (*Diary*, 746).

I do not fear anything, although the storm is raging, and frightful bolts strike all around me, and I then feel quite alone. Yet, my heart senses You, and my trust grows, and I see all Your omnipotence which upholds me (*Diary*, 761).

Turn With Trust To The Divine Mercy

I know the full power of Your mercy, and I trust that You will give me everything Your feeble child needs (*Diary*, 898).

† Oh, how ardently I desire that all mankind turn with trust to Your mercy. Then, seeing the glory of Your name, my heart will be comforted (*Diary*, 929).

† The soul gives the greatest glory to its Creator when it turns with trust to The Divine Mercy (*Diary*, 930).

I Am A Royal Child

† There are moments when I mistrust myself, when I feel my own weakness and wretchedness in the most profound depths of my own being, and I have noticed that I can endure such moments only by trusting in the infinite mercy of God (*Diary*, 944).

† I am going forward through life amidst rainbows and storms, but with my head held high with pride, for I am a royal child. I feel that the blood of Jesus is circulating in my veins, and I have put my trust in the great mercy of the Lord (*Diary*, 992).

A PLEDGE OF MERCY FOR SOULS

I feel that I am being completely transformed into prayer in order to beg God's mercy for every soul. O my Jesus, I am receiving You into my heart as a pledge of mercy for souls (*Diary*, 996).

I often receive light and the knowledge of the interior life of God and of God's intimate disposition, and this fills me with unutterable trust and a joy that I cannot contain within myself; I desire to dissolve completely in Him (*Diary*, 1102).

Jesus Is Full Of Mercy

When my soul is in anguish, I think only in this way: Jesus is good and full of mercy, and even if the ground were to give way under my feet, I would not cease to trust in Him (*Diary*, 1192).

All for You, Jesus. I desire to adore Your mercy with every beat of my heart, to the extent that I am able, to encourage souls to trust in that mercy, as You Yourself have commanded me, O Lord (*Diary*, 1234).

I Want To Become A Saint

I want to tell souls of Your goodness and encourage them to trust in Your mercy. That is my mission, which You Yourself have entrusted to me, O Lord, in this life and in the life to come (*Diary*, 1325).

Profound silence engulfs my soul. Not a single cloud hides the sun from me. I lay myself entirely open to its rays, that His love may effect a complete transformation in me. I want to come out of this retreat a saint, and this, in spite of everything; that is to say, in spite of my wretchedness, I want to become a saint, and I trust that God's mercy can make a saint even out of such misery as I am, because I am utterly in good will (*Diary*, 1333).

TRUST IN THE POWER OF YOUR GRACE

As I was praying before the Blessed Sacrament and greeting the five wounds of Jesus, at each salutation I felt a torrent of graces gushing into my soul, giving me a foretaste of heaven and absolute confidence in God's mercy (*Diary*, 1337).

O Lord, deify my actions so that they will merit eternity; although my weakness is great, I trust in the power of Your grace, which will sustain me (*Diary*, 1371).

I Depend On God

I live from one hour to the next and am not able to get along in any other way. I want to make the best possible use of the present moment, faithfully accomplishing everything that it gives me. In all things, I depend on God with unwavering trust (*Diary*, 1400).

† The better I have come to know my own misery, the stronger has become my trust in God's mercy (*Diary*, 1406).

You Surpass All Mothers

† Beyond all abandonment I trust, and in spite of my own feeling I trust, and I am being completely transformed into trust — often in spite of what I feel (*Diary*, 1489).

Above all things, I trust in You, Jesus, for You are unchangeable. My moods change, but You are always the same, full of mercy (*Diary*, 1489).

I entrust myself to You as a little child does to its mother's love. Even if all things were to conspire against me, and even if the ground were to give way under my feet, I would be at peace close to Your heart. You are always a most tender mother to me, and You surpass all mothers (*Diary*, 1490).

TOTAL TRUST IN HIM

† Even if I had had the sins of the whole world, as well as the sins of all the condemned souls weighing on my conscience, I would not have doubted God's goodness but, without hesitation, would have thrown myself into the abyss of The Divine Mercy, which is always open to us; and, with a heart crushed to dust, I would have cast myself at His feet, abandoning myself totally to His holy will, which is mercy itself (*Diary*, 1552).

There came to me a true knowledge of myself. Jesus is giving me a lesson in deep humility and, at the same time, one of total trust in Him. My heart is reduced to dust and ashes, and even if all people were to trample me under their feet, I would still consider that a favor (*Diary*, 1559).

You Are The God Of Mercy

Although my misery is great, and my offenses are many, I trust in Your mercy, because You are the God of mercy; and, from time immemorial, it has never been heard of, nor do heaven or earth remember, that a soul trusting in Your mercy has been disappointed (*Diary*, 1730).

When I received Jesus, I threw myself into Him as into an abyss of unfathomable mercy. And the more I felt I was misery itself, the stronger grew my trust in Him (*Diary*, 1817).

Mercy

January 18 - February 16

"Mercy is the second name of love" (John Paul II, Encyclical *Rich in Mercy*). Divine Mercy is God's love poured out in creating us, in redeeming us, and in sanctifying us. Divine Mercy is God's love poured out upon the unlovable and upon the unforgivable. Saint Faustina describes God as Love and Mercy itself. Another way to describe mercy is "love in action."

A mnemonic can describe MERCY:
Mighty Eternal Redeeming Compassionate Yahweh.

The Father is "rich in mercy," the Son is Mercy Incarnate making the Father *present as love and mercy*, and the Holy Spirit is mercy personified (John Paul II, Encyclical *Lord and Giver of Life*).

The following gems of St. Faustina are a challenge to us to trust in God's mercy and to ask for mercy on us and on the whole world, which is so in need of Divine Mercy.

THE IMMENSITY OF YOUR MERCY

The knowledge of my own misery allows me,
at the same time, to know the immensity of Your
mercy. In my own interior life, I am looking with
one eye at the abyss of my misery and baseness,
and with the other, at the abyss of Your mercy,
O God (*Diary*, 56).

O my Jesus, despite the deep night that is all
around me and the dark clouds which hide the
horizon, I know that the sun never goes out.
O Lord, though I cannot comprehend You and
do not understand Your ways, I nonetheless
trust in Your mercy (*Diary*, 73).

I Thank You For Your Great Mercy

I will show my gratitude unceasingly to God
for His great mercy towards me (*Diary*, 224).

The more miserable my soul is, the more
I feel the ocean of God's mercy engulfing me
and giving me strength and great power
(*Diary*, 225).

Thank You, Jesus, for the great favor of
making known to me the whole abyss of my
misery. I know that I am an abyss of nothingness
and that, if Your holy grace did not hold me up,
I would return to nothingness in a moment.
And so, with every beat of my heart, I thank You,
my God, for Your great mercy towards me
(*Diary*, 256).

You Are Compassion Itself

O my God, even in the punishments You send down upon the earth I see the abyss of Your mercy, for by punishing us here on earth You free us from eternal punishment (*Diary*, 423).

O God, You are compassion itself for the greatest sinners who sincerely repent. The greater the sinner, the greater his right to God's mercy (*Diary*, 423).

I desire to go throughout the whole world and speak to souls about the great mercy of God (*Diary*, 491).

The Crown Of Your Works

Mercy is the crown of Your works; You provide for all with the love of a most tender mother (*Diary*, 505).

If we live in this spirit of mercy, we ourselves will obtain mercy (*Diary*, 550).

Happy is the soul that calls upon the mercy of the Lord (*Diary*, 598).

$\mathcal{P}$RAISE THE LORD'S MERCY

All you souls, praise the Lord's mercy by trusting in His mercy all your life and especially at the hour of your death (*Diary*, 598).

And fear nothing, dear soul, whoever you are; the greater the sinner, the greater his right to Your mercy, O Lord (*Diary*, 598).

O Jesus, I wish to glorify Your mercy on behalf of thousands of souls. I know very well, O my Jesus, that I am to keep telling souls about Your goodness, about Your incomprehensible mercy (*Diary*, 598).

Mercy Is The Flower Of Love

I trust in You, O merciful God, and I wish to be the first to manifest to You that confidence which You demand of souls (*Diary*, 615).

Mercy is the flower of love. God is love, and mercy is His deed. In love it is conceived; in mercy it is revealed. Everything I look at speaks to me of God's mercy. Even God's very justice speaks to me about His fathomless mercy, because justice flows from love (*Diary*, 651).

Of myself I am nothing, and in my misery I have nothing of worth; so I abandon myself into the ocean of Your mercy, O Lord (*Diary*, 668).

*T*HE WEAPON OF MERCY

O Jesus, I understand that Your mercy is beyond all imagining, and therefore I ask You to make my heart so big that there will be room in it for the needs of all the souls living on the face of the earth (*Diary*, 692).

O Savior of the world. I unite myself with Your mercy. My Jesus, I join all my sufferings to Yours and deposit them in the treasury of the Church for the benefit of souls (*Diary*, 740).

I shall fight all evil with the weapon of mercy (*Diary*, 745).

THE SEAL OF YOUR MERCY

The mercy of the Lord is praised by the holy souls in heaven who have themselves experienced that infinite mercy. What these souls do in heaven, I already will begin to do here on earth (*Diary*, 753).

O my Jesus, teach me to open the bosom of mercy and love to everyone who asks for it. Jesus, my Commander, teach me so that all my prayers and deeds may bear the seal of Your mercy (*Diary*, 755).

O my Jesus, transform me into Yourself by the power of Your love, that I may be a worthy tool in proclaiming Your mercy (*Diary*, 783).

*P*OUR YOURSELF OUT UPON US!

Hide me, Jesus, in the depths of Your mercy,
and then let my neighbor judge me as he pleases
(*Diary*, 791).

You are a bottomless sea of mercy for us sinners;
and the greater the misery, the more right we have
to Your mercy (*Diary*, 793).

† O inexhaustible spring of Divine Mercy, pour
Yourself out upon us! Your Goodness knows no
limits (*Diary*, 819).

Who will ever conceive and understand the depth
of mercy that has gushed forth from Your Heart?
(*Diary*, 832).

THE FOUNT OF GOD'S MERCY

O God of fathomless mercy, who allow me to give relief and help to the dying by my unworthy prayer, be blessed as many thousand times as there are stars in the sky and drops of water in all the oceans! (*Diary*, 835).

† O human souls, where are you going to hide on the day of God's anger: Take refuge now in the fount of God's mercy. O what a great multitude of souls I see! They worshiped The Divine Mercy and will be singing the hymn of praise for all eternity (*Diary*, 848).

THE FULL POWER OF YOUR MERCY

O Jesus, have mercy! Embrace the whole world and press me to Your Heart. ... O Lord, let my soul repose in the sea of Your unfathomable mercy (*Diary*, 869).

My soul is in a sea of suffering. Sinners have taken everything away from me. But that is all right; I have given everything away for their sake that they might know that You are good and infinitely merciful (*Diary*, 893).

I know the full power of Your mercy, and I trust that You will give me everything Your feeble child needs (*Diary*, 898).

I OFFER EVERYTHING FOR SINNERS

Jesus, give me the souls of sinners; let Your mercy rest upon them. Take everything away from me, but give me souls. I want to become a sacrificial host for sinners (*Diary*, 908).

"Jesus, I offer everything today for sinners. Let the blows of Your justice fall on me, and the sea of Your mercy engulf the poor sinners" (*Diary*, 927).

The soul gives the greatest glory to its Creator when it turns with trust to The Divine Mercy (*Diary*, 930).

The Promise Of Mercy

I often accompany a person who is dying far away, but my greatest joy is when I see the promise of mercy fulfilled in these souls (*Diary*, 935).

There are moments when I mistrust myself, when I feel my own weakness and wretchedness in the most profound depths of my own being, and I have noticed that I can endure such moments only by trusting in the infinite mercy of God (*Diary*, 944).

The Love of God is the flower — Mercy the fruit (*Diary*, 948).

Constantly United With Him

I am constantly united with Him, and I am fully aware that I live for souls in order to bring them to Your mercy, O Lord. In this matter, no sacrifice is too insignificant (*Diary*, 971).

I am going forward through life amidst rainbows and storms, but with my head held high with pride, for I am a royal child. I feel that the blood of Jesus is circulating in my veins, and I have put my trust in the great mercy of the Lord (*Diary*, 992).

Take Advantage Of Mercy

I feel that I am being completely transformed into prayer in order to beg God's mercy for every soul. O my Jesus, I am receiving You into my heart as a pledge of mercy for souls (*Diary*, 996).

Let the glory and praise to The Divine Mercy rise from every creature throughout all ages and times (*Diary*, 1005).

Oh, how much we should pray for the dying! Let us take advantage of mercy while there is still time for mercy (*Diary*, 1035).

*H*IS FATHOMLESS MERCY

I realize more and more how much every soul needs God's mercy throughout life and particularly at the hour of death (*Diary*, 1036).

We resemble God most when we forgive our neighbors. God is Love, Goodness, and Mercy ... (*Diary*, 1148).

And my path is to be faithful to the will of God in all things and at all times, especially by being faithful to inner inspirations in order to be a receptive instrument in God's hands for the carrying out of the work of His fathomless mercy (*Diary*, 1173).

I Desire To Adore Your Mercy

God of unfathomable mercy, embrace the whole world and pour Yourself out upon us through the merciful Heart of Jesus (*Diary*, 1183).

All for You, Jesus. I desire to adore Your mercy with every beat of my heart and, to the extent that I am able, to encourage souls to trust in that mercy, as You Yourself have commanded me, O Lord (*Diary*, 1234).

Mercy For Every Soul

My Jesus, penetrate me through and through so that I might be able to reflect You in my whole life. Divinize me so that my deeds may have supernatural value. Grant that I may have love, compassion, and mercy for every soul without exception (*Diary*, 1242).

O my Jesus, each of Your saints reflects one of Your virtues; I desire to reflect Your compassionate heart, full of mercy; I want to glorify it. Let Your mercy, O Jesus, be impressed upon my heart and soul like a seal, and this will be my badge in this and the future life. Glorifying Your mercy is the exclusive task of my life (*Diary*, 1242).

The Abyss Of Your Mercy

I live in the deepest peace, because the Lord Himself is carrying me in the hollow of His hand. He, Lord of unfathomable mercy, knows that I desire Him alone in all things, always and everywhere (*Diary*, 1264).

At that moment, a ray of light illumined my soul, and I saw the whole abyss of my misery. In that same moment I nestled close to the Most Sacred Heart of Jesus with so much trust that even if I had the sins of all the damned weighing on my conscience, I would not have doubted God's mercy but, with a heart crushed to dust, I would have thrown myself into the abyss of Your mercy (*Diary*, 1318).

*T*ELL SOULS OF YOUR GOODNESS

I want to tell souls of Your goodness and encourage them to trust in Your mercy. That is my mission, which You Yourself have entrusted to me, O Lord, in this life and in the life to come (*Diary*, 1325).

Profound silence engulfs my soul. Not a single cloud hides the sun from me. I lay myself entirely open to its rays, that His love may effect a complete transformation in me. I want to come out of this retreat a saint, and this, in spite of everything; that is to say, in spite of my wretchedness, I want to become a saint, and I trust that God's mercy can make a saint even out of such misery as I am, because I am utterly in good will (*Diary*, 1333).

GREAT IS HIS MERCY!

As I was praying before the Blessed Sacrament and greeting the five wounds of Jesus, at each salutation I felt a torrent of graces gushing into my soul, giving me a foretaste of heaven and absolute confidence in God's mercy (*Diary*, 1337).

Nothing disturbs the depths of my peace. With one eye, I gaze on the abyss of my misery and with the other, on the abyss of Your mercy (*Diary*, 1345).

I would like to cry out to the whole world, "Love God, because He is good and great is His mercy!" (*Diary*, 1372).

My Trust In God's Mercy

The better I have come to know my own misery, the stronger has become my trust in God's mercy (*Diary*, 1406).

Oh, how great is the mercy of God, who allows man to participate in such a high degree in His divine happiness! At the same time, what great pain pierces my heart [at the thought] that so many souls have spurned this happiness (*Diary*, 1439).

O my Master, I surrender myself completely to You, who are the rudder of my soul; steer it Yourself according to Your divine wishes. I enclose myself in Your most compassionate Heart, which is a sea of unfathomable mercy (*Diary*, 1450).

THE MYSTERIES OF YOUR MERCY

Above all things, I trust in You, Jesus, for You are unchangeable. My moods change, but You are always the same, full of mercy (*Diary*, 1489).

† O incomprehensible God, my heart dissolves in joy that You have allowed me to penetrate the mysteries of Your mercy! Everything begins with Your mercy and ends with Your mercy (*Diary*, 1506).

All grace flows from mercy, and the last hour abounds with mercy for us. Let no one doubt concerning the goodness of God; even if a person's sins were as dark as night, God's mercy is stronger than our misery (*Diary*, 1507).

A Ray Of God's Merciful Grace

One thing alone is necessary: that the sinner set ajar the door of his heart, be it ever so little, to let in a ray of God's merciful grace, and then God will do the rest (*Diary*, 1507).

O merciful Lord, it is only out of mercy that You have lavished these gifts upon me. Seeing all these free gifts within me, with deep humility I worship Your incomprehensible goodness (*Diary*, 1523).

Always Open To Every Soul

Even if I had had the sins of the whole world,
as well as the sins of all the condemned souls
weighing on my conscience, I would not have
doubted God's goodness but, without hesitation,
would have thrown myself into the abyss of The
Divine Mercy, which is always open to us; and,
with a heart crushed to dust, I would have cast
myself at His feet, abandoning myself totally to
His holy will, which is mercy itself (*Diary*, 1552).

O my Jesus, Life of my soul, my Life, my Savior,
my sweetest Bridegroom, and at the same time my
Judge, You know that in this last hour of mine I do
not count on any merits of my own, but only on
Your mercy. Even as of today,
I immerse myself totally in the
abyss of Your mercy, which is
always open to every soul
(*Diary*, 1553).

The Depths Of Your Tender Mercy

O my Jesus, I have only one task to carry out in my lifetime, in death, and throughout eternity, and that is to adore Your incomprehensible mercy. No mind, either of angel or of man, will ever fathom the mysteries of Your mercy, O God (*Diary*, 1553).

The angels are lost in amazement before the mystery of Divine Mercy, but cannot comprehend it. Everything that has come from the Creator's hand is contained in this inconceivable mystery; that is to say, in the very depths of His tender mercy (*Diary*, 1553).

Anticipate Us With Your Grace

O Greatly Merciful God, Infinite Goodness, today all mankind calls out from the abyss of its misery to Your mercy — to Your compassion, O God; and it is with its mighty voice of misery that it cries out. Gracious God, do not reject the prayer of this earth's exiles! (*Diary*, 1570).

O Lord, Goodness beyond our understanding, who are acquainted with our misery through and through, and know that by our own power we cannot ascend to You, we implore You: anticipate us with Your grace and keep on increasing Your mercy in us, that we may faithfully do Your holy will all through our life and at death's hour (*Diary*, 1570).

THE CONSTANT MIRACLE OF YOUR MERCY

I do not know what to admire in You first: Your gentleness, Your hidden life, the emptying of Yourself for the sake of man, or the constant miracle of Your mercy, which transforms souls and raises them up to eternal life (*Diary*, 1584).

What I talk to You about, Jesus, is our secret, which creatures shall not know and Angels dare not ask about. These are secret acts of forgiveness, known only to Jesus and me; this is the mystery of His mercy, which embraces each soul separately (*Diary*, 1692).

I GLORIFY YOUR MERCY

O Christ, to the last moment of my life, I will not stop glorifying Your goodness and mercy. With every drop of my blood, with every beat of my heart, I glorify Your mercy. I long to be entirely transformed into a hymn of Your glory (*Diary*, 1708).

Although my misery is great, and my offenses are many, I trust in Your mercy, because You are the God of mercy; and, from time immemorial, it has never been heard of, nor do heaven or earth remember, that a soul trusting in Your mercy has been disappointed (*Diary*, 1730).

*T*HE TABERNACLE OF YOUR MERCY

May Your mercy be glorified, O Lord; we will praise it for endless ages. And the angels were amazed at the greatness of the mercy which You have shown for mankind ... (*Diary*, 1743).

On leaving the earth, O Lord, You wanted to stay with us, and so You left us Yourself in the Sacrament of the Altar, and You opened wide Your mercy to us. There is no misery that could exhaust You; You have called us all to this fountain of love, to this spring of God's compassion. Here is the tabernacle of Your mercy, here is the remedy for all our ills (*Diary*, 1747).

Misery

February 17 - 29

Misery is the one word that describes our present human condition. Certainly St. Faustina was aware of her own misery apart from the mercy of God, but the Lord also taught her even more about the nature of her own misery. One day she was thanking the Lord for the many graces given to her. She renewed the offering of herself to the Lord:

> I have given myself entirely to You; I have then nothing more that I can offer You. Jesus said to me, **My daughter, you have not offered Me that which is really yours.** I probed deeply into myself and found that I love God with all the faculties of my soul and, unable to see what it was that I had not yet given to the Lord, I asked, "Jesus, tell me what it is, and I will give it to You at once with a generous heart." Jesus said to me with kindness, **Daughter, give Me your misery, because it is your exclusive property** (*Diary*, 1318).

The response continues with a gem! (see February 25, *Diary*, 1318). She concludes her response with: "I believe, O Jesus, that You would not reject me, but would absolve me through the hand of Your representative" (*Diary*, 1318).

Earlier in her *Diary*, St. Faustina wrote: "The greater the misery, the greater right we have to Your mercy" (see February 23, *Diary*, 793). What great hope we have in God's mercy! Let us join with St. Faustina in giving Jesus all of our misery.

*H*ow Weak I am

The knowledge of my own misery allows me,
at the same time, to know the immensity of Your
mercy. In my own interior life, I am looking with
one eye at the abyss of my misery and baseness,
and with the other, at the abyss of Your mercy,
O God (*Diary*, 56).

O Jesus, You know how weak I am; be then
ever with me; guide my actions and my whole
being, You who are my very best Teacher!
(*Diary*, 66).

O Divine Sun, in Your rays the soul sees the
tiniest specks of dust which displease You
(*Diary*, 71).

$\mathcal{A}$ Beggar and Misery Itself

O my Jesus, despite the deep night that is all around me and the dark clouds which hide the horizon, I know that the sun never goes out. O Lord, though I cannot comprehend You and do not understand Your ways, I nonetheless trust in Your mercy (*Diary*, 73).

How can this be; You are God and I — I am Your creature. You, the Immortal King and I, a beggar and misery itself! But now all is clear to me; Your grace and Your love, O Lord, will fill the gulf between You, Jesus, and me (*Diary*, 199).

THE WHOLE ABYSS OF MY MISERY

The more miserable my soul is, the more I feel the ocean of God's mercy engulfing me and giving me strength and great power (*Diary*, 225).

Thank You, Jesus, for the great favor of making known to me the whole abyss of my misery. I know that I am an abyss of nothingness and that, if Your holy grace did not hold me up, I would return to nothingness in a moment. And so, with every beat of my heart, I thank You, my God, for Your great mercy towards me (*Diary*, 256).

MISERABLE AND SMALL

I want to love You as no human soul has ever loved You before; and although I am utterly miserable and small, I have nevertheless cast the anchor of my trust deep down into the abyss of Your mercy, O my God and Creator! In spite of my great misery I fear nothing, but hope to sing You a hymn of glory for ever (*Diary*, 283).

My happiest moments are when I am alone with my Lord. During these moments I experience the greatness of God and my own misery (*Diary*, 289).

Without You, I Am Nothing

Jesus, Eternal Light, enlighten my mind, strengthen my will, inflame my heart and be with me as You have promised, for without You I am nothing. You know, Jesus, how weak I am. I do not need to tell You this, for You Yourself know perfectly well how wretched I am. It is in You that all my strength lies (*Diary*, 495).

All my nothingness is drowned in the sea of Your mercy. With the confidence of a child, I throw myself into Your arms, O Father of Mercy, to make up for the unbelief of so many souls who are afraid to trust in You (*Diary*, 505).

You Yourself Direct My Affairs

Love casts out fear. Since I came to love God with my whole being and with all the strength of my heart, fear has left me (*Diary*, 589).

My Jesus, You see how weak I am of myself. Therefore, You Yourself direct my affairs. And know, Jesus, that without You I will not budge for any cause, but with You I will take on the most difficult things (*Diary*, 602).

I feel in my soul an unfathomable abyss which only God can fill. I lose myself in Him as a drop does in the ocean. The Lord has inclined Himself to my misery like a ray of the sun upon a barren and rocky desert (*Diary*, 605).

TAKE REFUGE IN THE FOUNT OF GOD'S MERCY

Of myself I am nothing, and in my misery I have nothing of worth; so I abandon myself into the ocean of Your mercy, O Lord (*Diary*, 668).

You are a bottomless sea of mercy for us sinners; and the greater the misery, the more right we have to Your mercy. You are a fount which makes all creatures happy by Your infinite mercy (*Diary*, 793).

O human souls, where are you going to hide on the day of God's anger? Take refuge now in the fount of God's mercy. O what a great multitude of souls I see! They worshiped The Divine Mercy and will be singing the hymn of praise for all eternity (*Diary*, 848).

THE WHOLE MISERY OF EXILE

My heart, longing for God, feels the whole misery of exile. I keep going forward bravely — though my feet become wounded — to my homeland and, on the way, I nourish myself on the will of God (*Diary*, 886).

I know the full power of Your mercy, and I trust that You will give me everything Your feeble child needs (*Diary*, 898).

Moments When I Mistrust Myself

There are moments when I mistrust myself,
when I feel my own weakness and wretchedness
in the most profound depths of my own being,
and I have noticed that I can endure such
moments only by trusting in the infinite mercy
of God (*Diary*, 944).

At that moment, a ray of light illumined my soul,
and I saw the whole abyss of my misery. In that
same moment I nestled close to the Most Sacred
Heart of Jesus with so much trust that even if I
had the sins of all the damned weighing on my
conscience, I would not have doubted God's mercy
but, with a heart crushed to dust, I would have
thrown myself into the abyss of Your mercy
(*Diary*, 1318).

*I*N SPITE OF MY WRETCHEDNESS

Profound silence engulfs my soul. Not a single cloud hides the sun from me. I lay myself entirely open to its rays, that His love may effect a complete transformation in me. I want to come out of this retreat a saint, and this, in spite of everything; that is to say, in spite of my wretchedness, I want to become a saint, and I trust that God's mercy can make a saint even out of such misery as I am, because I am utterly in good will (*Diary*, 1333).

Nothing disturbs the depths of my peace. With one eye, I gaze on the abyss of my misery and with the other, on the abyss of Your mercy (*Diary*, 1345).

ALL MANKIND CALLS OUT

He gave me a deeper knowledge of my own wretchedness. However, this great misery of mine does not deprive me of trust. On the contrary, the better I have come to know my own misery, the stronger has become my trust in God's mercy (*Diary*, 1406).

O Greatly Merciful God, Infinite Goodness, today all mankind calls out from the abyss of its misery to Your mercy — to Your compassion, O God; and it is with its mighty voice of misery that it cries out. Gracious God, do not reject the prayer of this earth's exiles! (*Diary*, 1570).

*F*ORTIFY THE POWERS OF MY SOUL

O Lord, Goodness beyond our understanding, who are acquainted with our misery through and through, and know that by our own power we cannot ascend to You, we implore You: anticipate us with Your grace and keep on increasing Your mercy in us, that we may faithfully do Your holy will all through our life and at death's hour (*Diary*, 1570).

Jesus, fortify the powers of my soul that the enemy gain nothing. Without You, I am weakness itself. What am I without Your grace if not an abyss of my own misery? Misery is my possession (*Diary*, 1630).

Although my misery is great, and my offenses are many, I trust in Your mercy, because You are the God of mercy; and, from time immemorial, it has never been heard of, nor do heaven or earth remember, that a soul trusting in Your mercy has been disappointed (*Diary*, 1730).

I Saw My Own Misery

One day during Holy Mass, the Lord gave me a deeper knowledge of His holiness and His majesty, and at the same time I saw my own misery. This knowledge made me happy, and my soul drowned itself completely in His mercy. I felt enormously happy (*Diary*, 1801).

I long for the time when God will come to my heart. I throw myself in His arms and tell Him about my inability and my misery. I pour out all the pain of my heart, for not being able to love Him as much as I want. I arouse within myself acts of faith, hope, and charity and live on that throughout the day (*Diary*, 1813).

When I had received Jesus in Holy Communion, my heart cried out with all its might, "Jesus, transform me into another host! I want to be a living host for You. You are a great and all-powerful Lord; You can grant me this favor" (*Diary*, 1826).

God's Will

March 1 - 22

The fundamental disposition of St. Faustina and of all the saints was their humble obedience to the will of God. Specific to the spirituality of St. Faustina was her trust in the mercy of God. In the final oblation of her life, she wrote: "Lead me, O God, along whatever roads You please; I have placed all my trust in Your will which is, for me, love and mercy itself" (Act of Oblation, 1937, *Diary*, 1264).

She expresses her uniqueness by her trust in the will of God, which is mercy and love itself — taught to her by the Blessed Mother (see *Diary*, 1244) and our Lord who told her to tell all people: **"That I am Love and Mercy itself."** (*Diary*, 1074).

Inspired by St. Faustina's example, let us seek God's will for our lives.

TRANSFORM ME COMPLETELY INTO YOURSELF

"Do with me as You please. I subject myself to Your will. As of today, Your holy will shall be my nourishment, and I will be faithful to Your commands with the help of Your grace" (*Diary*, 136).

Lord, transform me completely into Yourself, maintain in me a holy zeal for Your glory, give me the grace and spiritual strength to do Your holy will in all things (*Diary*, 240).

True love of God consists in carrying out God's will. To show God our love in what we do, all our actions, even the least, must spring from our love of God (*Diary*, 279).

JOINING OUR WILL TO THE WILL OF GOD

† From today on, I do the will of God everywhere, always, and in everything (*Diary*, 374).

Now I understand well that what unites our soul most closely to God is self-denial; that is, joining our will to the will of God. This is what makes the soul truly free, contributes to profound recollection of the spirit, and makes all life's burdens light, and death sweet (*Diary*, 462).

*R*ULE ME

I desire nothing but to fulfill God's desires. Lord, here are my soul and my body, my mind and my will, my heart and all my love. Rule me according to Your eternal plans (*Diary*, 492).

I will follow Your will insofar as You will permit me to do so through Your representative. O my Jesus, it cannot be helped, but I give priority to the voice of the Church over the voice with which You speak to me (*Diary*, 497).

*H*IS HOLY WILL

He [Jesus] told me that the most perfect and holy soul is the one that does the will of the Father, but there are not many such, and that He looks with special love upon the soul who lives His will (*Diary*, 603.)

Nothing will deter me from doing the will of God (*Diary*, 615).

I am not counting on my own strength, but on His omnipotence for, as He gave me the grace of knowing His holy will, He will also grant me the grace of fulfilling it (*Diary*, 615).

Do With Me As You Please

Our love for God consists in; namely, in doing
His will (*Diary*, 616).

Jesus, drive away from me the thoughts that
are not in accord with Your will. I know that
nothing now binds me to this earth but this
work of mercy (*Diary*, 638).

Despite the fears and qualms of my nature,
I am fulfilling Your holy will and desire to fulfill
it as faithfully as possible throughout my life and
in my death. Jesus, with You I can do all things.
Do with me as You please; only give me Your
merciful Heart and that is enough for me
(*Diary*, 650).

My Daily Food

† There is one word I heed and continually ponder; it alone is everything to me; I live by it and die by it, and it is the holy will of God. It is my daily food. My whole soul listens intently to God's wishes (_Diary_, 652).

I understood that all striving for perfection and all sanctity consist in doing God's will. Perfect fulfillment of God's will is maturity in sanctity; there is no room for doubt here (_Diary_, 666).

*P*UTTING YOUR WILL INTO PRACTICE

An extraordinary peace entered my soul when I reflected on the fact that, despite great difficulties, I had always faithfully followed God's will as I knew it. O Jesus, grant me the grace to put Your will into practice as I have come to know it, O God (*Diary*, 666).

The essence of the virtues is the will of God. He who does the will of God faithfully, practices all the virtues. In all the events and circumstances of my life, I adore and bless the holy will of God. The holy will of God is the object of my love. In the most secret depths of my soul, I live according to His will. I act exteriorly according to what I recognize inwardly as the will of God (*Diary*, 678).

FAITHFUL SUBMISSION TO THE WILL OF GOD

Jesus, Life and Truth, my Master, guide every step of my life, that I may act according to Your holy will (*Diary*, 688).

Faithful submission to the will of God, always and everywhere, in all events and circumstances of life, gives great glory to God (*Diary*, 724).

Such submission to the will of God carries more weight with Him than long fasts, mortifications, and the most severe penances (*Diary*, 724).

Totally In Accord With Your Will

Oh, how great is the reward for one act of loving submission to the will of God! (*Diary*, 724).

For my part, I have done everything, and it is now Your turn, my Jesus, and in this way Your cause will be made apparent. I am totally in accord with Your will; do with me as You please, O Lord, but only grant me the grace of loving You more and more ardently (*Diary*, 751).

† My goal is God ... and my happiness is in accomplishing His will, and nothing in the world can disturb this happiness for me: no power, no force of any kind (*Diary*, 775).

Nourished On The Will Of God

Transform me into Yourself and make me capable of doing Your holy will in all things and of returning Your love (*Diary*, 832).

My heart, longing for God, feels the whole misery of exile. I keep going forward bravely — though my feet become wounded — to my homeland and, on the way, I nourish myself on the will of God (*Diary*, 886).

Adorned With The Grace Of God

I have discovered a fountain of happiness in my soul, and it is God. O my God, I see that everything that surrounds me is filled with God, and most of all my own soul, which is adorned with the grace of God (*Diary*, 887).

Before we go to our Homeland, we must fulfill the will of God on earth; that is, trials and struggles must run their full course in us (*Diary*, 897).

*F*OR AS LONG AS YOU WISH

If it is Your will that I still go on living and suffering, then I desire what You have destined for me. Keep me here on earth for as long as You wish, even though this be until the end of the world (*Diary*, 918).

I am dying of the desire to be united with You forever, and You do not let death come near me. O will of God, you are the nourishment and delight of my soul. When I submit to the holy will of my God, a deep peace floods my soul (*Diary*, 952).

ℱROM A HIGHER POINT OF VIEW

The knowledge of God's will came to me; that is to say, I now see everything from a higher point of view and accept all events and things, pleasant and unpleasant, with love, as tokens of the heavenly Father's special affection (*Diary*, 956).

I understood that these two years of interior suffering which I have undergone in submission to God's will in order to know it better have advanced me further in perfection than the previous ten years (*Diary*, 981).

GOD NEVER VIOLATES OUR FREE WILL

My sanctity and perfection consist in the close union of my will with the will of God. God never violates our free will. It is up to us whether we want to receive God's grace or not. It is up to us whether we will cooperate with it or waste it (*Diary*, 1107).

And my path is to be faithful to the will of God in all things and at all times, especially by being faithful to inner inspirations in order to be a receptive instrument in God's hands for the carrying out of the work of His fathomless mercy (*Diary*, 1173).

*L*IVE IN THE PRESENT MOMENT

O Jesus, I want to live in the present moment, to live as if this were the last day of my life. I want to use every moment scrupulously for the greater glory of God, to use every circumstance for the benefit of my soul. I want to look upon everything, from the point of view that nothing happens without the will of God (*Diary*, 1183).

Jesus gave me to know that even the smallest thing does not happen on earth without His will (*Diary*, 1262).

I Desire You Alone

I desire to come out of this retreat a saint, even though human eyes will not notice this, not even those of the superiors. I abandon myself entirely to the action of Your grace. Let Your will be accomplished entirely in me, O Lord (*Diary*, 1326).

O Lord, You who penetrate my whole being and the most secret depths of my soul, You see that I desire You alone and long only for the fulfillment of Your holy will, paying no heed to difficulties or sufferings or humiliations or to what others might think (*Diary*, 1360).

*L*OVING CONSENT TO YOUR HOLY WILL

I submit myself completely and with loving consent to Your holy will, O Lord, and to Your most wise decrees, which are always full of clemency and mercy for me, though at times I can neither understand nor fathom them. O my Master, I surrender myself completely to You, who are the rudder of my soul; steer it Yourself according to Your divine wishes. I enclose myself in Your most compassionate Heart, which is a sea of unfathomable mercy (*Diary*, 1450).

Nothing happens by accident (*Diary*, 1530).

Abandoning Myself Totally To His Will

O Lord, if Your holy will has not yet been entirely fulfilled in me, here I am, ready for everything that You want, O Lord! (*Diary*, 1539).

Even if I had had the sins of the whole world, as well as the sins of all the condemned souls weighing on my conscience, I would not have doubted God's goodness but, without hesitation, would have thrown myself into the abyss of The Divine Mercy, which is always open to us; and, with a heart crushed to dust, I would have cast myself at His feet, abandoning myself totally to His holy will, which is mercy itself (*Diary*, 1552).

I Desire To Fulfill Your Holy Will

O my Jesus, my Master, I unite my desires to
the desires that You had on the Cross: I desire to
fulfill Your holy will; I desire the conversion of
souls; I desire that Your mercy be adored; I desire
that the triumph of the Church be hastened; I
desire the Feast of Mercy to be celebrated all
over the world; I desire sanctity for priests;
I desire that there be a saint in our Congregation
(*Diary*, 1581).

I do not know how to describe all that I suffer,
and what I have written thus far is merely a drop.
There are moments of suffering about which I
really cannot write. But there are
also moments in my life when
my lips are silent, and there are
no words for my defense, and
I submit myself completely to
the will of God (*Diary*, 1656).

In A Mysterious Manner

The Lord acts toward me in a mysterious manner. There are times when He Himself allows terrible sufferings, and then again there are times when He does not let me suffer and removes everything that might afflict my soul. These are His ways, unfathomable and incomprehensible to us (*Diary*, 1656).

It is for us to submit ourselves completely to His holy will. There are mysteries that the human mind will never fathom here on earth; eternity will reveal them (*Diary*, 1656).

An Interior Light

He gave me an interior light by which I learned that not a single word was mine; despite difficulties and adversities, I have always, always, fulfilled His will, as He has made it known to me (*Diary*, 1667).

Oh, how much I desire to be set free from the bonds of this body. O my Jesus, You know that, in all my desires, I always want to see Your will. Of myself, I would not want to die one minute sooner, or to live one minute longer, or to suffer less, or to suffer more, but I only want to do Your holy will (*Diary*, 1729).

A Constant Effort

This life of mine is a ceaseless struggle, a constant effort to do Your holy will; but may everything that is in me, both my misery and my strength, give praise to You, O Lord (*Diary*, 1740).

I have come to know that, in order for God to act in a soul, it must give up acting on its own; otherwise, God will not carry out His will in it (*Diary*, 1790).

St. Faustina's Heart

March 23 - April 5

The heart of St. Faustina was united completely with the Heart of Jesus. Her great abiding desire was to live every beat of her heart in union with the Heart of Jesus. Her "gems" show how her heart is a model for our desire to be one Heart with Jesus, so we can be a channel of His mercy to others.

During our "Divine Mercy Minutes" over the next couple of weeks, may this be our constant prayer of the heart to the Lord Jesus. As St. Faustina put it in addressing Jesus, "Your Heart is mine and mine is Yours alone" (*Diary*, 239).

A Little Cell In My Heart

I set up a little cell in my heart where I
always kept company with Jesus (*Diary*, 16).

My heart is a permanent dwelling place
for Jesus (*Diary*, 193).

Union with Jesus on the day of perpetual vows.
Jesus, from now on Your Heart is mine, and
mine is Yours alone (*Diary*, 239).

I WILL FORGIVE WITH ALL MY HEART

I will comfort the most sweet Eucharistic Heart continuously and will play harmonious melodies on the strings of my heart. Suffering is the most harmonious melody of all (*Diary*, 385).

He who knows how to forgive prepares for himself many graces from God. As often as I look upon the Cross, so often will I forgive with all my heart (*Diary*, 390).

Your Pure Love Has Entered My Heart

O Jesus, my heart stops beating when I think of all You are doing for me! I am amazed at You, Lord, that You would stoop so low to my wretched soul! What inconceivable means You take to convince me! (*Diary*, 460)

O Jesus! I sense keenly how Your divine Blood is circulating in my heart; I have not the least doubt that Your most pure love has entered my heart with Your most sacred Blood (*Diary*, 478).

*T*HE LITTLE HEAVEN OF MY HEART

O my God, I have come to know You within
my heart, and I have loved You above all things
that exist on earth or in heaven. Our hearts
have a mutual understanding, and no one of
humankind will comprehend this (*Diary*, 478).

Jesus, when You come to me in Holy Communion,
You who together with the Father and the Holy
Spirit have deigned to dwell in the little heaven
of my heart, I try to keep You company
throughout the day, I do not leave You
alone for even a moment (*Diary*, 486).

Great Happiness Fills My Heart

When I am asleep I offer Him every beat of my heart; when I awaken I immerse myself in Him without saying a word (*Diary*, 486).

Oh, what great happiness fills my heart from knowing God and the divine life! It is my desire to share this happiness with all people. I cannot keep this happiness locked in my own heart alone, for His flames burn me and cause my bosom and my entrails to burst asunder (*Diary*, 491).

*I*NFLAME MY HEART

Jesus, Eternal Light, enlighten my mind, strengthen my will, inflame my heart and be with me as You have promised, for without You I am nothing. You know, Jesus, how weak I am. I do not need to tell You this, for You yourself know perfectly well how wretched I am. It is in You that all my strength lies (*Diary,* 495).

Jesus, make my heart like unto Yours, or rather transform it into Your own Heart that I may sense the needs of other hearts, especially those who are sad and suffering. May the rays of mercy rest in my heart (*Diary,* 514).

DYING OF LONGING FOR YOU

"I beg You for only one thing: to make my heart capable of loving You" (*Diary,* 587).

"You know very well, Jesus, that my heart is dying of longing for You. Everything that is not You is nothing to me" (*Diary,* 587).

O Jesus, I understand that Your mercy is beyond all imagining, and therefore I ask You to make my heart so big that there will be room in it for the needs of all the souls living on the face of the earth (*Diary,* 692).

Make My Heart Like Unto Your Heart

My Jesus, make my heart like unto Your merciful Heart. Jesus, help me to go through life doing good to everyone (*Diary*, 692).

With my heart I encompass the whole world, especially countries which are uncivilized or where there is persecution. I am praying for mercy upon them (*Diary*, 742).

I must seek only the advice of my confessor. I must always have a heart which is open to receive the sufferings of others, and drown my own sufferings in the Divine Heart so that they would not be noticed on the outside, in so far as possible (*Diary*, 792).

Everyone Has A Place In My Heart

O most sweet Jesus who, in Your incomprehensible kindness, have deigned to unite my wretched heart to Your most merciful Heart, it is with Your own Heart that I glorify God, our Father, as no soul has ever glorified Him before (*Diary*, 836).

My heart is always open to the sufferings of others; and I will not close my heart to the sufferings of others, even though because of this I have been scornfully nicknamed "dump"; that is, [because] everyone dumps his pain into my heart. [To this] I answered that everyone has a place in my heart and I, in return, have a place in the Heart of Jesus (*Diary*, 871).

O Treasure Of My Heart

Oh, how ardently I desire that all mankind turn
with trust to Your mercy. Then, seeing the glory
of Your name, my heart will be comforted
(*Diary*, 929).

My heart wants nothing but You alone,
O Treasure of my heart. For all the gifts
You give me, thank you, O Lord, but I
desire only Your Heart (*Diary*, 969).

ℰ Pledge Of Mercy For Souls

I feel that I am being completely transformed
into prayer in order to beg God's mercy for
every soul. O my Jesus, I am receiving You
into my heart as a pledge of mercy for souls
(*Diary*, 996).

In You my soul drowns, in You my heart dissolves.
I know not how to love partially, but only with
the full strength of my soul and the total ardor
of my heart. You Yourself, O Lord, have enkindled
this love of mine for You; in You my heart has
drowned forever (*Diary*, 1030).

Silence In My Heart

I strive for silence in my heart amidst the greatest
sufferings, and I protect myself against all attacks
with the shield of Your Name (*Diary*, 1040).

My heart is languishing for God. I desire to
become united with Him. A faint fear pierces
my soul and at the same time a kind of flame
of love sets my heart on fire. Love and
suffering are united in my heart (*Diary*, 1050).

*W*ITH EVERY BEAT OF MY HEART

There is no greater happiness than when
God gives me to know interiorly that every
beat of my heart is pleasing to Him, and when
He shows me that He loves me in a special way
(*Diary*, 1121).

All for You, Jesus. I desire to adore Your mercy
with every beat of my heart and, to the extent
that I am able, to encourage souls to trust in
that mercy, as You Yourself have commanded
me, O Lord (*Diary*, 1234).

Υou Come To My Heart

No one can conceive the happiness which my heart enjoys in its solitude, alone with God (*Diary,* 1395).

† Jesus, there is one more secret in my life, the deepest and dearest to my heart: it is You Yourself when You come to my heart under the appearance of bread. Herein lies the whole secret of my sanctity. Here my heart is so united with Yours as to be but one. There are no more secrets, because all that is Yours is mine, and all that is mine is Yours (*Diary,* 1489).

The greater the graces which my heart receives, the deeper it plunges itself in humility (*Diary,* 1661).

Struggle, Satan, Spiritual Warfare

April 6 - 19

Saint Faustina soon learned "that Satan hates mercy more than anything else. It is his greatest torment" (*Diary*, 764). With the grace of God for support, St. Faustina waged a mighty war against the forces of darkness. In the midst of battle, her armor against Satan was God's mercy. She found that sometimes it was good "to flee for cover in the wound of the Heart of Jesus" (*Diary*, 145).

May understanding how St. Faustina struggled against Satan encourage us when we are under spiritual attack.

*H*ARD-FOUGHT BATTLES

A soul that is united with God must be prepared for great and hard-fought battles (*Diary*, 121).

There are attacks when a soul has no time to think or seek advice; then it must enter into a life-or-death struggle. Sometimes it is good to flee for cover in the wound of the Heart of Jesus, without answering a single word (*Diary*, 145).

THE HUMBLE ARE STRONG

Satan defeats only the proud and the cowardly, because the humble are strong (*Diary*, 450).

My Jesus, despite Your graces, I see and feel all my misery. I begin my day with battle and end it with battle. As soon as I conquer one obstacle, ten more appear to take its place. But I am not worried, because I know that this is the time of struggle, not peace (*Diary*, 606).

Your Omnipotence Upholds Me

When the burden of the battle becomes
too much for me, I throw myself like a child
into the arms of the heavenly Father and trust
I will not perish (*Diary*, 606).

I do not fear anything, although the storm
is raging, and frightful bolts strike all around
me, and I then feel quite alone. Yet, my heart
senses You, and my trust grows, and I see all
Your omnipotence which upholds me
(*Diary*, 761).

Mercy — Satan's Greatest Torment

The greater the difficulties which I see, the more am I at peace. Oh, if in this whole matter the glory of God and the profit to souls were not greatly served, Satan would not be opposing it so much (*Diary*, 764).

† I have now learned that Satan hates mercy more than anything else. It is his greatest torment (*Diary*, 764).

I Have Fought A Battle

Today I have fought a battle with the spirits
of darkness over one soul. How terribly Satan
hates God's mercy! I see how he opposes
this whole work (*Diary*, 812).

Although the desert is fearful, I walk with
lifted head and eyes fixed on the sun; that
is to say, on the merciful Heart of Jesus
(*Diary*, 886).

*P*ERIODS OF BATTLE

When it happens that the living presence
of God, which [a soul that loves God] enjoys
almost constantly, leaves [the soul], she then tries to
continue living in lively faith. Her soul
understands that there are periods of rest
and periods of battle (*Diary*, 890).

Before we go to our Homeland, we must
fulfill the will of God on earth; that is, trials
and struggles must run their full course in us
(*Diary*, 897).

*F*IXING MY GAZE UPON THE CROSS

In difficult moments, I will fix my gaze upon
the silent Heart of Jesus, stretched upon the Cross,
and from the exploding flames of His merciful
Heart, will flow down upon me power and
strength to keep fighting (*Diary*, 906).

† Satan can even clothe himself in a cloak of
humility, but he does not know how to wear the
cloak of obedience and thus his evil designs will
be disclosed (*Diary*, 939).

'You Can Do All Things'

When I see that the burden is beyond my strength, I do not consider or analyze it or probe into it, but I run like a child to the Heart of Jesus and say only one word to Him: "You can do all things." And then I keep silent, because I know that Jesus Himself will intervene in the matter, and as for me, instead of tormenting myself, I use that time to love Him (*Diary*, 1033).

I strive for silence in my heart amidst the greatest sufferings, and I protect myself against all attacks with the shield of Your Name (*Diary*, 1040).

*N*OT CEASING TO TRUST IN HIM

In spite of the profound peace my soul is
enjoying, I am struggling continuously, and
it is often a hard-fought battle for me to walk
faithfully along my path; that is, the path which
the Lord Jesus wants me to follow (*Diary*, 1173).

When my soul is in anguish, I think only
in this way: Jesus is good and full of mercy,
and even if the ground were to give way
under my feet, I would not cease to trust
in Him (*Diary*, 1192).

Hide Me In Your Mercy

I know well that the greater and the more
beautiful the work is, the more terrible will
be the storms that rage against it (*Diary*, 1401).

Jesus, hide me in Your mercy and shield me
against everything that might terrify my soul.
Do not let my trust in Your mercy be disappointed.
Shield me with the omnipotence of Your mercy,
and judge me leniently as well (*Diary*, 1480).

STRENGTH FOR BATTLE

"Jesus, I ask You, give me the strength for battle. Let it be done to me according to Your most holy will. My soul is enamored of Your most holy will" (*Diary*, 1498).

There are no indifferent moments in my life, since every moment of my life is filled with prayer, suffering, and work. If not in one way, then in another, I glorify God; and if God were to give me a second life, I do not know whether I would make better use of it ... (*Diary*, 1545).

Jesus, Save Me!

I spent the whole night with Jesus in Gethsemane. From my breast there escaped one continuous moan. A natural dying will be much easier, because then one is in agony and will die; while here, one is in agony, but cannot die. O Jesus, I never thought such suffering could exist. Nothingness: that is the reality. O Jesus, save me! I believe in You with all my heart (*Diary*, 1558).

The glory of The Divine Mercy is resounding, even now, in spite of the efforts of its enemies and of Satan himself, who has a great hatred for God's mercy (*Diary*, 1659).

FIGHT AGAINST MY ENEMIES

The enemy's greatest efforts will not
thwart the smallest detail of what the
Lord has decreed (*Diary*, 1659).

I strive to be faithful to God and to love
Him to the point of complete forgetfulness
of self. And He Himself looks after me and
fights against my enemies (*Diary*, 1720).

THE DIVINE MERCY WILL TRIUMPH

This life of mine is a ceaseless struggle,
a constant effort to do Your holy will; but may
everything that is in me, both my misery and my
strength, give praise to You, O Lord (_Diary,_ 1740).

In spite of Satan's anger, The Divine Mercy will
triumph over the whole world and will be
worshiped by all souls (_Diary,_ 1789).

Union with God

April 20 - May 3

For St. Faustina, perfection consisted in close union with God (see *Diary*, 457). She described this union as a drop of water immersed in the ocean (see *Diary*, 432). This union with God is a foretaste of heaven on earth, and this grace is available by simple faithfulness to God (see *Diary*, 507). Saint Faustina could even say, "My spirit communicates with God without any word being spoken. I am aware that He is living in me and I in Him" (*Diary*, 560).

Let us do what we can in our own lives to strive for a closer union with God.

I Am Never Alone

I absorb God into myself in order to
give Him to souls (*Diary*, 193).

I am never alone, because [God] is my
constant companion. He is present to me
at every moment. Our intimacy is very close,
through a union of blood and of life (*Diary*, 318).

I know that I am united with Him as
closely as a drop of water is united with
the bottomless ocean (*Diary*, 411).

God Dwells Within Me

I feel powerless in the embrace of God.
I feel that I am in Him and that I am
dissolved in Him like a drop of water
in the ocean (*Diary*, 432).

I look for no happiness beyond my
own interior where God dwells. I rejoice
that God dwells within me; here I abide
with Him unendingly; it is here that my
greatest intimacy with Him exists (*Diary*, 454).

Perfection consists in this close union
with God (*Diary*, 457).

THE CLOSEST UNION WITH GOD

Now I understand well that what unites
our soul most closely to God is self-denial;
that is, joining our will to the will of God.
This is what makes the soul truly free, contributes
to profound recollection of the spirit, and makes all
life's burdens light, and death sweet (*Diary,* 462).

The silent soul is capable of attaining
the closest union with God. It lives almost
always under the inspiration of the Holy Spirit.
God works in a silent soul without hindrance
(*Diary,* 477).

A Union That Is Extraordinary

I unite myself closely with Jesus and stand before Him as an atoning sacrifice on behalf of the world. God will refuse me nothing when I entreat Him with the voice of His Son (*Diary*, 482).

Already here on earth we can taste the happiness of those in heaven by an intimate union with God, a union that is extraordinary and often quite incomprehensible to us. One can attain this very grace through simple faithfulness of soul (*Diary*, 507).

$\mathcal{H}$E IS LIVING IN ME

† My spirit communicates with God without any word being spoken. I am aware that He is living in me and I in Him (*Diary*, 560).

No exterior thing hinders my union with God (*Diary*, 582).

I recognized the purpose and destiny of my life. My purpose is to become closely united to God through love, and my destiny is to praise and glorify God's mercy (*Diary*, 729).

*L*ONGING FOR HIM

Jesus, my spirit yearns for You, and I
desire very much to be united with You,
but Your works hold me back. The number
of souls that I am to bring to You is not yet
complete (*Diary*, 761).

I desire only God Himself, and yet
I must live. This is a martyrdom beyond
description. God imparts Himself to the
soul in a loving way and draws it into the
infinite depths of His divinity, but at the
same time He leaves it here on earth for
the sole purpose that it might suffer and
die of longing for Him (*Diary*, 856).

*L*OVE ALONE EXPLAINS OUR UNION

You are the Creator and I am Your creature, nevertheless, love alone explains our union (*Diary,* 885).

† I don't know how to live without [Jesus]. I would rather be with Him in afflictions and suffering than without Him in the greatest heavenly delights (*Diary,* 912).

My Jesus, in spite of everything, I desire very much to unite myself to You. Jesus, if this be possible, take me to Yourself, for it seems to me that my heart will burst of longing for You! (*Diary,* 918).

Completely Drowned In His Greatness

I am constantly united with Him, and
I am fully aware that I live for souls in order
to bring them to Your mercy, O Lord. In this
matter, no sacrifice is too insignificant
(*Diary*, 971).

Today, the Majesty of God enveloped
and transpierced my soul to its very depths.
The greatness of God is pervading my being
and flooding me so that I am completely
drowning in His greatness. I am dissolving
and disappearing entirely in Him as in my
life-source, as in perfect life (*Diary*, 983).

*L*ANGUISHING FOR GOD

† My heart is languishing for God. I desire to become united with Him. A faint fear pierces my soul and at the same time a kind of flame of love sets my heart on fire. Love and suffering are united in my heart (*Diary,* 1050).

† If a soul loves God sincerely and is intimately united with Him, then, even though such a soul may be living in the midst of difficult external circumstances, nothing can disturb its interior life (*Diary,* 1094).

*L*IVING IN CLOSE INTIMACY WITH GOD

My sanctity and perfection consist in the close union of my will with the will of God. God never violates our free will. It is up to us whether we want to receive God's grace or not. It is up to us whether we will cooperate with it or waste it (*Diary*, 1107).

What happiness it is to have the consciousness of God in one's heart and to live in close intimacy with Him (*Diary*, 1135).

*I*ntense Hunger For God

I experienced such intense hunger for God that I seemed to be dying of the desire to become united with Him (*Diary*, 1186).

My soul is shrouded in suffering. I am continually uniting myself to [God] by an act of the will. He is my power and strength (*Diary*, 1207).

A TABERNACLE FOR THE LIVING HOST

My soul is filled with God's light and nourishes itself from Him. My feelings are as if dead. This is a purely spiritual union with God; it is a great predominance of spirit over nature (*Diary*, 1278).

My heart is a living tabernacle in which the living Host is reserved. I have never sought God in some far-off place, but within myself. It is in the depths of my own being that I commune with my God (*Diary*, 1302).

THE SERAPHIC SOULS

My God, despite all the graces, I long without cease to be eternally united with my God; and the better I know Him, the more ardently I desire Him (*Diary*, 1303).

Among [God's] chosen ones, there are some who are especially chosen, and whom He calls to a higher form of holiness, to exceptional union with Him. These are seraphic souls, from whom God demands greater love than He does from others (*Diary*, 1556).

I Converse With The Lord

O my Jesus, I know that, in order to be useful to souls, one has to strive for the closest possible union with You, who are Eternal Love. One word from a soul united to God effects more good in souls than eloquent discussions and sermons from an imperfect soul (*Diary*, 1595).

The moments which are most pleasant to me are those when I converse with the Lord within the center of my being. I try my very best not to leave Him alone. He likes to be always with us ... (*Diary*, 1793).

Love

May 4 - June 7

Saint Faustina could not stop marveling at how much God loves us (see *Diary*, 1292). She wanted to cry out to the whole world, "Love God, because He is good and great is His mercy" (*Diary*, 1372). She learned that the purest and most concentrated love is sacrifice and suffering.

The great Apostle of Divine Mercy came to realize, "Truth wears a crown of thorns" (*Diary*, 1103). Yet, it was in the very midst of such pain and suffering that she recognized opportunities to show her love for God. She observed, "When we suffer much we have a great chance to show God that we love Him" (*Diary*, 303).

May we, too, through everything that we do, show God how much we love Him.

*P*URE LOVE

I came to know how very much God
loves me (*Diary*, 16).

O my Lord, inflame my heart with love
for You, that my spirit may not grow weary
amidst the storms, the sufferings, and
the trials (*Diary*, 94).

Pure love is capable of great deeds, and
it is not broken by difficulty or adversity
(*Diary*, 140).

Only One Thing Is Needed

Only one thing is needed to please God:
to do even the smallest things out of great love —
love, and always love (*Diary*, 140).

If [a soul's] love is great, Jesus now makes
it known that it is time to put into action
what it has received (*Diary*, 145).

THE MORE FIERCELY I LOVE HIM

How can this be; You are God and I —
I am Your creature. You, the Immortal
King and I, a beggar and misery itself!
But now all is clear to me; Your grace
and Your love, O Lord, will fill the gulf
between You, Jesus, and me (*Diary*, 199).

The more I come to know [God], the
more ardently, the more fiercely I love Him,
and the more perfect my acts become
(*Diary*, 231).

My Heart On The Paten

Today I place my heart on the paten where Your Heart has been placed, O Jesus, and today I offer myself together with You to God, Your Father and mine, as a sacrifice of love and praise. Father of Mercy, look upon the sacrifice of my heart, but through the wound in the Heart of Jesus (*Diary,* 239).

True love of God consists in carrying out God's will. To show God our love in what we do, all our actions, even the least, must spring from our love of God (*Diary,* 279).

Suffering For Love Of God

In my interior life I never reason; I do not analyze the ways in which God's Spirit leads me. It is enough for me to know that I am loved and that I love (*Diary*, 293).

† When we suffer much we have a great chance to show God that we love Him; but when we suffer little we have less occasion to show God our love; and when we do not suffer at all, our love is then neither great nor pure (*Diary*, 303).

PROOF OF MY LOVE FOR HIM

Love must be reciprocal. If Jesus tasted the fullness of bitterness for me, then I, His bride, will accept all bitterness as proof of my love for Him (*Diary,* 389).

O Jesus! I sense keenly how Your divine Blood is circulating in my heart; I have not the least doubt that Your most pure love has entered my heart with Your most sacred Blood (*Diary,* 478).

*H*OW MUCH I LOVE HOLY CHURCH

O my God, I have come to know You within
my heart, and I have loved You above all things
that exist on earth or in heaven (*Diary,* 478).

What a joy it is to be a faithful child of
the Church! Oh, how much I love Holy Church
and all those who live in it! I look upon them as
living members of Christ, who is their Head
(*Diary,* 481).

BURNING WITH LOVE

I burn with love with those who love; I suffer with those who suffer. I am consumed with sorrow at the sight of those who are cold and ungrateful; and I then try to have such a love for God that it will make amends for those who do not love Him, those who feed their Savior with ingratitude at its worst (*Diary*, 481).

The majesty of God overwhelmed me. I felt that I was immersed in God, totally immersed in Him and penetrated by Him, being aware of how much the heavenly Father loves us (*Diary*, 491).

*N*O GREATER JOY

Only love has meaning; it raises up our smallest actions into infinity (*Diary*, 502).

No greater joy is to be found than that of loving God (*Diary*, 507).

† The more I come to know Him, the more I desire to love Him. I burn with the desire to love Him ever more and more (*Diary*, 525).

*L*OVE CASTS OUT FEAR

I beg You for only one thing: to make my heart capable of loving you (*Diary*, 587).

Love casts out fear. Since I came to love God with my whole being and with all the strength of my heart, fear has left me (*Diary*, 589).

My Love For You Grows

O Lord, immerse my soul in the ocean
of Your divinity and grant me the grace of
knowing You; for the better I know You,
the more I desire You, and the more my love
for You grows (*Diary*, 605).

Our love for God consists in; namely, in
doing His will (*Diary*, 616).

Mercy is the flower of love. God is love,
and mercy is His deed. In love it is conceived;
in mercy it is revealed. Everything I look at
speaks to me of God's mercy. Even God's
very justice speaks to me about
His fathomless mercy, because
justice flows from love
(*Diary*, 651).

THE FIRE OF LIVING LOVE

I have enclosed myself in the tabernacle together with Jesus, my Master. He Himself drew me into the fire of living love on which everything converges (*Diary*, 704).

My love wants to equal the love of the Mighty One. It is drawn to Him so vehemently that it is impossible, without some special grace from God, to bear the vastness of such a grace in this life (*Diary*, 708).

I Drown In Him

Only love can understand this meeting
of two spirits, namely, God-who-is-Spirit
and the soul-who-is-creature. The more I
know Him, the more completely with all the
strength of my being I drown in Him
(*Diary*, 729).

There is but one thing that is of infinite
value in His eyes, and that is love of God;
love, love and once again, love; and nothing
can compare with a single act of pure love
of God. Oh, with what inconceivable
favors God gifts a soul that loves Him
sincerely! (*Diary*, 778).

How Much He Loves Me

O my Jesus, transform me into Yourself
by the power of Your love, that I may be
a worthy tool in proclaiming Your mercy
(*Diary*, 783).

Jesus, my Love, today gave me to
understand how much He loves me,
although there is such an enormous gap
between us, the Creator and the creature;
and yet, in a way, there is something like
equality: love fills up the gap. He Himself descends
to me and makes me capable of communing
with Him (*Diary*, 815).

To Love Him To Folly

Even if [Jesus] called me to Himself today, the work would not suffer at all by that, because He Himself is the Lord of both the work and the worker. My part is to love Him to folly; all works are nothing more than a tiny drop before Him. It is love that has meaning and power and merit (*Diary*, 822).

Transform me into Yourself and make me capable of doing Your holy will in all things and of returning Your love (*Diary*, 832).

*L*OVE — A TRANSFORMING MYSTERY

Only love makes it possible to understand
these incomprehensible intimacies with
which You visit me (*Diary*, 885).

Jesus, You have given me to know and
understand in what a soul's greatness consists:
not in great deeds but in great love (*Diary*, 889).

Love is a mystery that transforms everything
it touches into things beautiful and pleasing
to God (*Diary*, 890).

THE LOVING GAZE OF GOD

The love of God makes a soul free. She is like a queen; she knows no slavish compulsion; she sets about everything with great freedom of soul, because the love which dwells in her incites her to action. (*Diary*, 890)

A soul in love with God and immersed in Him approaches her duties with the same dispositions as she does Holy Communion and carries out the simplest tasks with great care, under the loving gaze of God (*Diary*, 890).

Astonished by God's Love

How greatly concerned I am for all mankind, that "they all do not know You, and those who do know You do not love You as You deserve to be loved" (*Diary*, 929).

Unending is my interior astonishment that the Most High Lord is pleased in me and tells me so Himself. And I immerse myself even deeper in my nothingness, because I know what I am of myself. Still I must say that I, in return, love my Creator to folly with every beat of my heart and with every nerve; my soul unconsciously drowns, drowns ... in Him (*Diary*, 947).

God's Love For The Suffering Soul

The Love of God is the flower —
Mercy the fruit (*Diary*, 948).

† Oh, if only the suffering soul knew
how it is loved by God, it would die of joy
and excess of happiness! Some day, we will
know the value of suffering, but then we
will no longer be able to suffer. The present
moment is ours (*Diary*, 963).

I very much desire to know God more
deeply and to love Him more ardently,
for I have understood that the greater
the knowledge, the stronger
the love (*Diary*, 974).

GREAT LOVE FOR YOU

My Jesus, I understand well that my perfection consists not in the fact that You command me to carry out these great works of Yours — Oh no! — the soul's greatness does not consist in this, but in great love for You (*Diary*, 984).

† O Jesus, in the depths of my soul I understand that the greatest achievements cannot compare with one act of pure love for You (*Diary*, 984).

THE FULL FORCE OF LOVE

† The greatest greatness is to love God;
true greatness is in loving God; real wisdom
is to love God (*Diary*, 990).

My heart has come to love the Lord with
the full force of love, and I know no other love,
because it is from the beginning that my soul has
sunk deeply in the Lord as in its only treasure
(*Diary*, 1021).

Even if the Lord were to hide, love will
know how to find Him (*Diary*, 1022).

The Total Ardor Of My Heart

† O my Jesus, give me wisdom, give me a mind great and enlightened by Your light, and this only, that I may know You better, O Lord. For the better I get to know You, the more ardently will I love You, the sole object of my love (*Diary*, 1030).

In You my soul drowns, in You my heart dissolves. I know not how to love partially, but only with the full strength of my soul and the total ardor of my heart. You Yourself, O Lord, have enkindled this love of mine for You; in You my heart has drowned forever (*Diary*, 1030).

Only Love Is Of Any Value

† I have come to know that only love is of any value; love is greatness; nothing, no works, can compare with a single act of pure love of God (*Diary,* 1092).

If a soul loves God sincerely and is intimately united with Him, then, even though such a soul may be living in the midst of difficult external circumstances, nothing can disturb its interior life (*Diary,* 1094).

† The quintessence of love is sacrifice and suffering. Truth wears a crown of thorns. Prayer involves the intellect, the will, and the emotions (*Diary,* 1103).

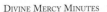

Enkindle In me The Fire Of God's Love

Before every Holy Communion I earnestly ask the Mother of God to help me prepare my soul for the coming of her Son, and I clearly feel her protection over me. I entreat her to be so gracious as to enkindle in me the fire of God's love, such as burned in her own pure heart at the time of the Incarnation of the Word of God (*Diary,* 1114).

I do not know how to live without God, but I also feel that God, absolutely self-sufficient though He is, cannot be happy without me ... (*Diary,* 1120).

*I*MMERSED IN LOVE

There is no greater happiness than when
God gives me to know interiorly that every
beat of my heart is pleasing to Him, and when
He shows me that He loves me in a special way
(*Diary*, 1121).

When my soul is immersed in love, I solve
the most intricate questions clearly and quickly.
Only love is able to cross over precipices and
mountain peaks. Love, once again, love
(*Diary*, 1123).

STRIVE FOR THE LOVE OF GOD

As long as we live, the love of God grows
in us. Until we die, we ought to strive for
the love of God (*Diary,* 1191).

My Jesus, penetrate me through and through
so that I might be able to reflect You in my
whole life. Divinize me so that my deeds may
have supernatural value. Grant that I may have
love, compassion, and mercy for every soul
without exception (*Diary,* 1242).

A Love So Great

I could not stop marveling at how much
God loves us (*Diary*, 1292).

† My Jesus, You know that from my earliest
years I have wanted to become a great saint;
that is to say, I have wanted to love You with
a love so great that there would be no soul
who has hitherto loved You so (*Diary*, 1372).

CRY OUT TO THE WHOLE WORLD

† I would like to cry out to the whole world,
"Love God, because He is good and great
is His mercy!" (*Diary*, 1372).

God loves in a special way those whom
we love (*Diary*, 1438).

The Sweetness Of God's Love

"Jesus, give me an intellect, a great intellect, for this only, that I may understand You better; because the better I get to know You, the more ardently will I love You" (*Diary,* 1474).

I am all immersed in love; I love and feel that I am loved, and with full consciousness I experience this. My soul is drowning in the Lord, realizing the great Majesty of God and its own littleness; but through this knowledge my happiness increases ... This awareness is so vivid in the soul, so powerful and, at the same time, so sweet (*Diary,* 1500).

$\mathcal{P}$URE FLAME

Everlasting love, pure flame, burn in my heart
ceaselessly and deify my whole being, according
to Your infinite pleasure by which You summoned
me into existence and called me to take part in
Your everlasting happiness (*Diary*, 1523).

† O merciful Lord, it is only out of mercy that
You have lavished these gifts upon me. Seeing
all these free gifts within me, with deep humility
I worship Your incomprehensible goodness
(*Diary*, 1523).

The Delight Of God's Love

Lord, my heart is filled with amazement that You, absolute Lord, in need of no one, would nevertheless stoop so low out of pure love for us. I can never help being amazed that the Lord would have such an intimate relationship with His creatures. That again is His unfathomable goodness (*Diary*, 1523).

What a delight it is to love with all the force of one's soul and to be loved even more in return, to feel and experience this with the full consciousness of one's being. There are no words to express this (*Diary*, 1523).

A Greater Degree Of Love

Among His chosen ones, there are some who are especially chosen, and whom He calls to a higher form of holiness, to exceptional union with Him. These are seraphic souls, from whom God demands greater love than He does from others (*Diary*, 1556).

He sometimes demands of a particular soul a greater degree of love. Such a soul understands this call, because God makes this known to it interiorly, but the soul may either follow this call or not. It depends on the soul itself whether it is faithful to these touches of the Holy Spirit, or whether it resists them (*Diary*, 1556).

$\mathcal{T}$EACH ME TO LOVE YOU

O Wound of Mercy, Heart of Jesus, hide me
in Your depths as a drop of Your own Blood,
and do not let me out forever! Lock me in Your
depths, and do You Yourself teach me to love You!
Eternal Love, do You Yourself form my soul that
it be made capable of returning Your love
(*Diary*, 1631).

O Christ, suffering for You is the delight
of my heart and my soul. Prolong my sufferings
to infinity, that I may give You a proof of my
love. I accept everything that Your hand will
hold out to me. Your love, Jesus, is enough for me
(*Diary*, 1662).

A New Flame Of Love

I strive to be faithful to God and to love Him to the point of complete forgetfulness of self. And He Himself looks after me and fights against my enemies (*Diary*, 1720).

I came to know the attributes of God. Burning with an inner fire of love, I went out to the garden to cool off; when I looked up at the heavens, a new flame of love flooded my heart (*Diary*, 1755).

TRANSFORMED INTO LOVE FOR YOU

O my Jesus, You know that I desire to
love You with a love that no soul has ever
before loved You with. I would like the whole
world to be transformed into love for You,
my Betrothed (*Diary*, 1771).

Today, I want to be transformed, whole
and entire, into the love of Jesus and to
offer myself, together with Him, to the
Heavenly Father (*Diary*, 1820).

Suffering

June 8 - 26

*H*ere are some startling insights that St. Faustina learned through uniting her suffering with the sufferings of Christ:

• "Suffering is the greatest treasure on earth" (*Diary*, 342).

• "Suffering is the thermometer which measures the love of God in a soul" (*Diary*, 774).

• Suffering gives us the power to save souls (see *Diary*, 735 and 1032).

• Chosen suffering souls "uphold the existence of mankind" (*Diary*, 926).

• "If only the suffering soul knew how it is loved by God, it would die of joy and excess of happiness!" (*Diary*, 963).

May these gems on suffering give you fresh insight into the mystery of suffering. May you never again waste the precious gift of your own suffering.

REFUGE IN THE LORD

My desires are mad and unattainable. I wish to conceal from You that I suffer. I want never to be rewarded for my efforts and my good actions. You Yourself, Jesus, are my only reward; You are enough, O Treasure of my heart! (*Diary*, 57).

When I feel that the suffering is more than I can bear, I take refuge in the Lord in the Blessed Sacrament, and I speak to Him with profound silence (*Diary*, 73).

Amidst The Sufferings

I see that God never tries us beyond
what we are able to suffer (*Diary*, 78).

O Jesus, I want to burn as a pure offering
and to be consumed before the throne of
Your hiddenness (*Diary*, 80).

O my Lord, inflame my heart with love
for You, that my spirit may not grow weary
amidst the storms, the sufferings, and
the trials (*Diary*, 94).

Suffer Without Complaining

Oh, how pleasing are the hymns flowing from a suffering soul! (*Diary,* 114).

Difficulties do not terrify [the soul]; they are its daily bread, as it were (*Diary,* 145).

To suffer without complaining, to bring comfort to others, and to drown my own sufferings in the most Sacred Heart of Jesus! (*Diary,* 224).

*C*HE DAILY FOOD OF MY SOUL

I have joined my sacrifice in a special way to the sacrifice of the crucified Jesus, in order to thus become more pleasing to God (*Diary,* 250).

† From the moment I came to love suffering, it ceased to be a suffering for me. Suffering is the daily food of my soul (*Diary,* 276).

† When we suffer much we have a great chance to show God that we love Him; but when we suffer little we have less occasion to show God our love; and when we do not suffer at all, our love is then neither great nor pure (*Diary,* 303).

THE GREATEST TREASURE ON EARTH

† Suffering is the greatest treasure on earth; it purifies the soul. In suffering, we learn who is our true friend (*Diary*, 342).

I will comfort the most sweet Eucharistic Heart continuously and will play harmonious melodies on the strings of my heart. Suffering is the most harmonious melody of all (*Diary*, 385).

In the sufferings of soul or body, I try to keep silence, for then my spirit gains the strength that flows from the Passion of Jesus (*Diary*, 487).

*U*NIMAGINABLE GLORY

In the midst of all sufferings, both physical and spiritual, as well as in darkness and desolation, I will remain silent, like a dove, and not complain (*Diary,* 504).

O my Jesus, Eternal Truth, I fear nothing, neither hardships nor sufferings; I fear only one thing, and that is to offend You. My Jesus, I would rather not exist than make You sad (*Diary,* 571).

The Lord also gave me to understand what unimaginable glory awaits the person who resembles the suffering Jesus here on earth. That person will resemble Jesus in His glory (*Diary,* 604).

$\mathcal{A}$ Martyrdom Beyond Description

I will enclose myself in the chalice of Jesus
so that I may comfort Him continually. I will
do everything within my power to save souls,
and I will do it through prayer and suffering
(*Diary*, 735).

In the spiritual life, suffering is the thermometer
which measures the love of God in a soul
(*Diary*, 774).

I desire only God Himself, and yet I must live.
This is a martyrdom beyond description. God
imparts Himself to the soul in a loving way and
draws it into the infinite depths of His divinity,
but at the same time He leaves it here on earth for
the sole purpose that it might suffer and die of
longing for Him (*Diary*, 856).

OPEN TO THE SUFFERINGS OF OTHERS

I suffer because of my longing for You,
O Lord. You have left me the Sacred Host,
O Lord, but it enkindles in my soul an even
greater longing for You, O my Creator and
Eternal God! Jesus, I yearn to become united
with You (*Diary*, 867).

† My heart is always open to the sufferings
of others; and I will not close my heart to the
sufferings of others, even though because of this
I have been scornfully nicknamed "dump"; that is,
[because] everyone dumps his pain into my heart.
[To this] I answered that everyone has a place in
my heart and I, in return, have
a place in the Heart of Jesus
(*Diary*, 871).

Chosen Souls Uphold The World

My soul is in a sea of suffering. Sinners have taken everything away from me, But that is all right; I have given everything away for their sake that they might know that You are good and infinitely merciful (*Diary*, 893).

I don't know how to live without [Jesus]. I would rather be with Him in afflictions and suffering than without Him in the greatest heavenly delights (*Diary*, 912).

The Lord gave me to know who it is that upholds the existence of mankind: it is the chosen souls. When the number of the chosen ones is complete, the world will cease to exist (*Diary*, 926).

THE OPEN WOUND OF THE HEART OF JESUS

† When great sufferings will cause my nature to tremble, and my physical and spiritual strength will diminish, then will I hide myself deep in the open wound of the Heart of Jesus, silent as a dove, without complaint (*Diary*, 957).

Oh, if only the suffering soul knew how it is loved by God, it would die of joy and excess of happiness! (*Diary*, 963).

† Some day, we will know the value of suffering, but then we will no longer be able to suffer. The present moment is ours (*Diary*, 963).

Love And Suffering United

I suffer great pain at the sight of the suffering of others. All these sufferings are reflected in my heart. I carry their torments in my heart so that it even wears me out physically. I would like all pains to fall upon me so as to bring relief to my neighbor (*Diary*, 1039).

I strive for silence in my heart amidst the greatest sufferings, and I protect myself against all attacks with the shield of Your Name (*Diary*, 1040).

My heart is languishing for God. I desire to become united with Him. A faint fear pierces my soul and at the same time a kind of flame of love sets my heart on fire. Love and suffering are united in my heart (*Diary*, 1050).

SHROUDED IN SUFFERING

† The quintessence of love is sacrifice
and suffering. Truth wears a crown of thorns
(*Diary*, 1103).

My soul is shrouded in suffering. I am
continually uniting myself to Him by an
act of the will. He is my power and strength
(*Diary*, 1207).

God often grants many and great graces
out of regard for the souls who are suffering,
and He withholds many punishments solely
because of the suffering souls (*Diary*, 1268).

Becoming Like Jesus

† The greater the sufferings, the more I see that I am becoming like Jesus. This is the surest way. If some other way were better, Jesus would have shown it to me (*Diary*, 1394).

† Sufferings in no way take away my peace. On the other hand, although I enjoy profound peace, that peace does not lessen my experience of suffering (*Diary*, 1394).

[Jesus] is bringing me to understand deeply how everything depends on His will, and how He allows certain difficulties precisely for our merit, so that our fidelity might be clearly manifest. And through this, I have been given strength for suffering and self-denial (*Diary*, 1409).

THANK YOU FOR THE CUP OF SUFFERING

Thank You in advance, O Lord, for everything Your goodness will send me. Thank You for the cup of suffering from which I shall daily drink. Do not diminish its bitterness, O Lord, but strengthen my lips that, while drinking of this bitterness, they may know how to smile for love of You, my Master (*Diary*, 1449).

† Jesus, do not leave me alone in suffering. You know, Lord, how weak I am. I am an abyss of wretchedness, I am nothingness itself; so what will be so strange if You leave me alone and I fall? I am an infant, Lord, so I cannot get along by myself (*Diary*, 1489).

No Indifferent Moments

Now that I have difficulty sleeping at night, because my suffering won't allow it, I visit all the churches and chapels and, if only for a brief moment, I make an act of adoration before the Blessed Sacrament (*Diary*, 1501).

There are no indifferent moments in my life, since every moment of my life is filled with prayer, suffering, and work. If not in one way, then in another, I glorify God; and if God were to give me a second life, I do not know whether I would make better use of it ... (*Diary*, 1545).

WITH YOU ON CALVARY

My Jesus, I now see that I have gone through all the stages of my life following You: childhood, youth, vocation, apostolic work, Tabor, Gethsemane, and now I am already with You on Calvary (*Diary,* 1580).

I cannot practice any greater mortifications, because I am so very weak. This long illness has sapped my strength completely. I am uniting myself with Jesus through suffering. When I meditate on His Painful Passion, my physical sufferings are lessened (*Diary,* 1625).

Emptying The Cup

O Christ, if my soul had known, all at once, what it was going to have to suffer during its lifetime, it would have died of terror at the very sight; it would not have touched its lips to the cup of bitterness. But as it has been given to drink a drop at a time, it has emptied the cup to the very bottom (*Diary*, 1655).

† My Jesus, You suffice me for everything else in the world. Although the sufferings are severe, You sustain me. Although the times of loneliness are terrible, You make them sweet for me. Although the weakness is great, You change it into power for me (*Diary*, 1655).

Silent Moments Of Suffering

I do not know how to describe all that I suffer,
and what I have written thus far is merely a drop.
There are moments of suffering about which I
really cannot write. But there are also moments
in my life when my lips are silent, and there are
no words for my defense, and I submit myself
completely to the will of God (*Diary*, 1656).

The Lord acts toward me in a mysterious
manner. There are times when He Himself
allows terrible sufferings, and then again there
are times when He does not let me suffer and
removes everything that might afflict my soul.
These are His ways, unfathomable and
incomprehensible to us
(*Diary*, 1656).

MAGNIFICENT GIFTS

O Christ, suffering for You is the delight of my heart and my soul. Prolong my sufferings to infinity, that I may give You a proof of my love. I accept everything that Your hand will hold out to me. Your love, Jesus, is enough for me (*Diary*, 1662).

My God, although my sufferings are great and protracted, I accept them from Your hands as magnificent gifts. I accept them all, even the ones that other souls have refused to accept. You can come to me with everything, my Jesus; I will refuse You nothing. I ask You for only one thing: give me the strength to endure them and grant that they may be meritorious. Here is my whole being; do with me as You please (*Diary*, 1795).

Desire

June 27 - July 18

*S*aint Faustina's desires for the Lord are expressed in some of the most sparkling gems of her *Diary*! She describes her "mad and unattainable" desires (*Diary*, 57). She wanted to go throughout the whole world to proclaim God's great mercy (see *Diary*, 491, 697, 793, 929, 1771). She felt she was dying of yearning for God (see *Diary*, 970, 1137).

Our desire for God is the key to our spiritual life and the key to entering into God's eternal and divine will. Our desire is so essential and fundamental because God in His great love for us respects our free will. He will not violate it. But when we desire His eternal will, He then can flood us with His gifts without destroying our freedom.

As we reflect on these gems, let's ask the Lord to stir in our hearts a greater desire to love and serve Him. Like St. Faustina, may we "burn with the desire to love [the Lord] ever more and more" (*Diary*, 525).

Mad And Unattainable

"Jesus, my Spouse, do You not see that
my soul is dying because of its longing
for You? How can You hide Yourself from
a heart that loves You so sincerely?" (*Diary*, 25).

† My desires are mad and unattainable.
I wish to conceal from You that I suffer.
I want never to be rewarded for my efforts
and my good actions. You Yourself, Jesus,
are my only reward; You are enough,
O Treasure of my heart! (*Diary*, 57).

Great Happiness

I desire to struggle, toil, and empty myself for our work of saving immortal souls (*Diary*, 194).

I feel dislike for all things that the world holds in esteem. With all my soul I desire silence and solitude (*Diary*, 432).

Oh, what great happiness fills my heart from knowing God and the divine life! It is my desire to share this happiness with all people. I cannot keep this happiness locked in my own heart alone, for His flames burn me and cause my bosom and my entrails to burst asunder (*Diary*, 491).

THE BURNING DESIRE TO LOVE HIM MORE

† I desire to go throughout the whole world
and speak to souls about the great mercy
of God (*Diary*, 491).

I desire nothing but to fulfill God's desires.
Lord, here are my soul and my body, my mind
and my will, my heart and all my love. Rule me
according to Your eternal plans (*Diary*, 492).

† The more I come to know [God], the more
I desire to love Him. I burn with the desire
to love Him ever more and more (*Diary*, 525).

*D*YING OF LONGING FOR YOU

"You know very well, Jesus, that my heart
is dying of longing for You. Everything that
is not You is nothing to me." (*Diary*, 587).

O my Jesus, the more I have known You,
the more ardently I have desired You (*Diary*, 591).

My God, I desire nothing but the fulfillment
of Your will. It does not matter whether it
will be easy or difficult (*Diary*, 615).

I Desire Nothing But Your Glory

Despite the fears and qualms of my nature, I am fulfilling Your holy will and desire to fulfill it as faithfully as possible throughout my life and in my death. Jesus, with You I can do all things (*Diary*, 650).

O God, You who pervade my soul, You know that I desire nothing but Your glory (*Diary*, 650).

I desire to glorify Your infinite mercy during my life, at the hour of death, in the resurrection, and throughout eternity (*Diary*, 697).

GREAT ARE MY DESIRES

Jesus, my spirit yearns for You, and I desire very much to be united with You, but Your works hold me back. The number of souls that I am to bring to You is not yet complete (*Diary*, 761).

† Great are my desires. I desire that all humankind come to know the Lord. I would like to prepare all nations for the coming of the Word Incarnate (*Diary*, 793).

I am surprised that it does not separate the soul from the body. I desire God; I want to become immersed in Him (*Diary*, 807).

The Yearning Of My Soul

O eternal God, how ardently I desire
to glorify this greatest of Your attributes;
namely, Your unfathomable mercy (*Diary*, 835).

Nothing can still the yearning of my soul.
I long for You, O my Creator and eternal God!
Neither celebrations nor beautiful hymns
soothe my soul; rather, they make me yearn
all the more. At the very mention of Your Name,
my spirit springs toward You, O Lord (*Diary*, 850).

DESIRING ONLY GOD HIMSELF

† I desire only God Himself, and yet I must live. This is a martyrdom beyond description. God imparts Himself to the soul in a loving way and draws it into the infinite depths of His divinity, but at the same time He leaves it here on earth for the sole purpose that it might suffer and die of longing for Him (*Diary*, 856).

I suffer because of my longing for You, O Lord. You have left me the Sacred Host, O Lord, but it enkindles in my soul an even greater longing for You, O my Creator and Eternal God! Jesus, I yearn to become united with You (*Diary*, 867).

*M*Y HEART BURSTS WITH LONGING FOR YOU

My heart, longing for God, feels the whole misery of exile. I keep going forward bravely — though my feet become wounded— to my homeland and, on the way, I nourish myself on the will of God (*Diary*, 886).

My Jesus, in spite of everything, I desire very much to unite myself to You. Jesus, if this be possible, take me to Yourself, for it seems to me that my heart will burst of longing for You! (*Diary*, 918).

DRAWING ASIDE THE VEILS OF HEAVEN

"Oh, how ardently I desire that all mankind turn with trust to Your mercy. Then, seeing the glory of Your name, my heart will be comforted" (*Diary*, 929).

I desire to draw aside the veils of heaven, so that the earth would have no doubts about The Divine Mercy (*Diary*, 930).

*M*AY YOUR HOLY WILL ALWAYS COME FIRST

Let all my desires, even the holiest, noblest, and most beautiful, take always the last place and Your holy will, the very first. The least of Your desires, O Lord, is more precious to me than heaven, with all its treasures (*Diary*, 957).

"My heart wants nothing but You alone, O Treasure of my heart. For all the gifts You give me, thank you, O Lord, but I desire only Your Heart" (*Diary*, 969).

I am dying of yearning for God (*Diary*, 970).

To Know God More Deeply

I very much desire to know God more deeply and to love Him more ardently, for I have understood that the greater the knowledge, the stronger the love (*Diary*, 974).

My heart is languishing for God. I desire to become united with Him. A faint fear pierces my soul and at the same time a kind of flame of love sets my heart on fire. Love and suffering are united in my heart (*Diary*, 1050).

To Dissolve Completely In Him

I often receive light and the knowledge of the interior life of God and of God's intimate disposition, and this fills me with unutterable trust and a joy that I cannot contain within myself; I desire to dissolve completely in Him (*Diary*, 1102).

† I am dying of yearning for God today. This longing fills all my soul. How very much I feel I am in exile. O Jesus, when will the longed-for moment come? (*Diary*, 1137).

To Adore Your Mercy

I experienced such intense hunger for God that I seemed to be dying of the desire to become united with Him (*Diary*, 1186).

† All for You, Jesus. I desire to adore Your mercy with every beat of my heart and, to the extent that I am able, to encourage souls to trust in that mercy, as You yourself have commanded me, O Lord (*Diary*, 1234).

I Desire Him Alone

† O my Jesus, each of Your saints reflects
one of Your virtues; I desire to reflect Your
compassionate heart, full of mercy; I want to
glorify it. Let Your mercy, O Jesus, be impressed
upon my heart and soul like a seal, and this
will be my badge in this and the future life.
Glorifying Your mercy is the exclusive task
of my life (*Diary*, 1242).

I live in the deepest peace, because the
Lord Himself is carrying me in the hollow
of His hand. He, Lord of unfathomable
mercy, knows that I desire Him alone in
all things, always and everywhere
(*Diary*, 1264).

*E*TERNALLY UNITED WITH MY GOD

† My God, despite all the graces, I long without cease to be eternally united with my God; and the better I know Him, the more ardently I desire Him (*Diary*, 1303).

I desire to come out of this retreat a saint, even though human eyes will not notice this, not even those of the superiors. I abandon myself entirely to the action of Your grace. Let Your will be accomplished entirely in me, O Lord (*Diary*, 1326).

I Want To Become A Saint

Profound silence engulfs my soul. Not a single cloud hides the sun from me. I lay myself entirely open to its rays, that His love may effect a complete transformation in me. I want to come out of this retreat a saint, and this, in spite of everything; that is to say, in spite of my wretchedness, I want to become a saint, and I trust that God's mercy can make a saint even out of such misery as I am, because I am utterly in good will (*Diary*, 1333).

In spite of all my defeats, I want to go on fighting like a holy soul and to comport myself like a holy soul. I will not be discouraged by anything, just as nothing can discourage a soul who is holy. I want to live and die like a holy soul, with my eyes fixed on You, Jesus, stretched out on the Cross, as the model for my actions (*Diary*, 1333).

The Best Of Guides

I used to look around me for examples and found nothing which sufficed, and I noticed that my state of holiness seemed to falter. But from now on, my eyes are fixed on You, O Christ, who are for me the best of guides. I am confident that You will bless my efforts (*Diary*, 1333).

O Lord, You who penetrate my whole being and the most secret depths of my soul, You see that I desire You alone and long only for the fulfillment of Your holy will, paying no heed to difficulties or sufferings or humiliations or to what others might think (*Diary*, 1360).

*U*NITING MY DESIRE TO YOURS

My God, I see the radiance of eternal dawn.
My whole soul bounds toward You, O Lord;
nothing any longer holds me back, nothing
ties me to earth (*Diary*, 1365).

O my Jesus, my Master, I unite my desires
to the desires that You had on the Cross: I desire
to fulfill Your holy will; I desire the conversion of
souls; I desire that Your mercy be adored; I desire
that the triumph of the Church be hastened; I
desire the Feast of Mercy to be celebrated all
over the world; I desire sanctity for priests;
I desire that there be a saint in our
Congregation (*Diary*, 1581).

Everything That My Heart Could Desire

O Wound of Mercy, Heart of Jesus, hide me in Your depths as a drop of Your own Blood, and do not let me out forever! Lock me in Your depths, and do You Yourself teach me to love You! Eternal Love, do You Yourself form my soul that it be made capable of returning Your love. O living Love, enable me to love You forever. I yearn to eternally reciprocate Your love (*Diary*, 1631).

My Lord and Creator, Your goodness encourages me to converse with You. Your mercy abolishes the chasm which separates the Creator from the creature. To converse with You, O Lord, is the delight of my heart. In You I find everything that my heart could desire (*Diary*, 1692).

I Desire To Be Set Free

Oh, how much I desire to be set free from
the bonds of this body. O my Jesus, You know
that, in all my desires, I always want to see
Your will. Of myself, I would not want to die
one minute sooner, or to live one minute longer,
or to suffer less, or to suffer more, but I only
want to do Your holy will (*Diary*, 1729).

† O my Jesus, You know that I desire to
love You with a love that no soul has ever
before loved You with. I would like the whole
world to be transformed into love for You,
my Betrothed (*Diary*, 1771).

I Pour Out All The Pain Of My Heart

I long for the time when God will come to my heart. I throw myself in His arms and tell Him about my inability and my misery (*Diary*, 1813).

I pour out all the pain of my heart, for not being able to love Him as much as I want. I arouse within myself acts of faith, hope, and charity and live on that throughout the day (*Diary*, 1813).

Knowledge of God

July 19 - 31

The more St. Faustina came to know God the more she came to love Him — and the more she loved God the more she wanted to know Him. It was an ever escalating spiral of knowledge and love that she experienced as she grew ever more united with Him: "The more I come to know Him, the more I desire to love Him" (*Diary*, 525). And again she wrote: "The more I come to know Him, the more ardently, the more fiercely I love Him, and the more perfect my acts become" (*Diary*, 231).

There is more, there is more, and there is ever so much more knowledge for us to discover about God! Like St. Faustina, may we always strive to deepen our knowledge of God, and thus seek to love Him more and more for who He truly is.

How Great You Are!

O God, the more I know You the less I can comprehend You, but this "non-comprehension" lets me realize how great You are! And it is this impossibility of comprehending You which enflames my heart anew for You (*Diary,* 57).

O my Jesus, You are the life of my life. You know only too well that I long for nothing but the glory of Your name and that souls come to know Your goodness (*Diary,* 57).

United Closely With The Spirit Of The Church

The more I come to know Him, the more
ardently, the more fiercely I love Him, and
the more perfect my acts become (*Diary*, 231).

Almost every feast of the Church gives
me a deeper knowledge of God and a
special grace. That is why I prepare myself
for each feast and unite myself closely with
the spirit of the Church (*Diary*, 481).

GREAT HAPPINESS FROM KNOWING GOD

Oh, what great happiness fills my heart from knowing God and the divine life! It is my desire to share this happiness with all people. I cannot keep this happiness locked in my own heart alone, for His flames burn Me and cause my bosom and my entrails to burst asunder (*Diary*, 491).

Priests, help me to proclaim [Jesus'] mercy, for every word falls short of how merciful He really is (*Diary*, 491).

Coming To Know Him

† The more I come to know Him, the more
I desire to love Him. I burn with the desire
to love Him ever more and more (*Diary*, 525).

And Jesus gave me to know that I should
ask Him more questions and seek His advice
(*Diary*, 560).

O my Jesus, the more I have known You,
the more ardently I have desired You
(*Diary*, 591).

Depth In The Knowledge Of God

O Holy Trinity, Eternal God, I thank You
for allowing me to know the greatness and
the various degrees of glory to which souls
attain. Oh, what a great difference of depth
in the knowledge of God there is between one
degree and another! (*Diary*, 605).

I am not counting on my own strength,
but on His omnipotence for, as He gave me
the grace of knowing His holy will, He will also
grant me the grace of fulfilling it (*Diary*, 615).

Knowing What Makes A Soul Great

Great are my desires. I desire that all humankind come to know the Lord. I would like to prepare all nations for the coming of the Word Incarnate (*Diary*, 793).

Who will ever conceive and understand the depth of mercy that has gushed forth from Your Heart? (*Diary*, 832).

† Jesus, You have given me to know and understand in what a soul's greatness consists: not in great deeds but in great love (*Diary*, 889).

KNOWING THE FULL POWER OF YOUR MERCY

I know the full power of Your mercy, and
I trust that You will give me everything
Your feeble child needs (*Diary*, 898).

I am coming to know God's greatness more
and more and to rejoice in Him. I remain
unceasingly with Him in the depths of my heart.
It is in my own soul that I most easily find God
(*Diary*, 903).

How greatly concerned I am for all mankind,
that "they all do not know You, and those who
do know You do not love You as You deserve
to be loved" (*Diary*, 929).

$\mathcal{K}$NOWLEDGE OF GOD'S WILL

The knowledge of God's will came to me; that is to say, I now see everything from a higher point of view and accept all events and things, pleasant and unpleasant, with love, as tokens of the heavenly Father's special affection (*Diary*, 956).

Oh, if only the suffering soul knew how it is loved by God, it would die of joy and excess of happiness! Some day, we will know the value of suffering, but then we will no longer be able to suffer. The present moment is ours (*Diary*, 963).

THE GREATER THE KNOWLEDGE, THE STRONGER THE LOVE

† I very much desire to know God more deeply and to love Him more ardently, for I have understood that the greater the knowledge, the stronger the love (*Diary*, 974).

I understood that these two years of interior suffering which I have undergone in submission to God's will in order to know it better have advanced me further in perfection than the previous ten years (*Diary*, 981).

GIVE ME WISDOM

† O my Jesus, give me wisdom, give me a mind great and enlightened by Your light, and this only, that I may know You better, O Lord. For the better I get to know You, the more ardently will I love You, the sole object of my love (*Diary*, 1030).

The Lord gave me to know how much He desires a soul to distinguish itself by deeds of love. And in spirit I saw how many souls are calling out to us, "Give us God." And the blood of the Apostles boiled up within me. I will not be stingy with it; I will shed it all to the last drop for immortal souls (*Diary*, 1249).

DEEPER KNOWLEDGE OF MY OWN WRETCHEDNESS

† My God, despite all the graces, I long without cease to be eternally united with my God; and the better I know Him, the more ardently I desire Him (*Diary*, 1303).

He gave me a deeper knowledge of my own wretchedness. However, this great misery of mine does not deprive me of trust. On the contrary, the better I have come to know my own misery, the stronger has become my trust in God's mercy (*Diary*, 1406).

KNOWING EVERYTHING DEPENDS ON HIS WILL

He is bringing me to understand deeply how everything depends on His will, and how He allows certain difficulties precisely for our merit, so that our fidelity might be clearly manifest. And through this, I have been given strength for suffering and self-denial (*Diary*, 1409).

"Jesus, give me an intellect, a great intellect, for this only, that I may understand You better; because the better I get to know You, the more ardently will I love You" (*Diary*, 1474).

$\mathcal{A}$ True Knowledge Of Myself

There came to me a true knowledge of myself. Jesus is giving me a lesson in deep humility and, at the same time, one of total trust in Him. My heart is reduced to dust and ashes, and even if all people were to trample me under their feet, I would still consider that a favor (*Diary,* 1559).

He gave me an interior light by which I learned that not a single word was mine; despite difficulties and adversities, I have always, always, fulfilled His will, as He has made it known to me (*Diary,* 1667).

Daily Life

August 1 - 10

The daily routine of work and monotony was a treasure for St. Faustina. She looked at each hour and every minute as a time for offering to the Lord her sufferings and her duties of the moment. She said, "These are no indifferent moments in my life, since every moment of my life is filled with prayer, suffering, and work" (*Diary*, 1545).

Saint Faustina's faithfulness to the Lord in daily life was an important and concrete way that she expressed her love for Him. She would make "small, everyday sacrifices" and strew them "like wild flowers" before the feet of her beloved Jesus (*Diary*, 208).

What daily sacrifices can we make to show our love for the Lord Jesus?

Small, Everyday Sacrifices

O life so dull and monotonous, how many treasures you contain! When I look at everything with the eyes of faith, no two hours are alike, and the dullness and monotony disappear (*Diary*, 62).

O you small, everyday sacrifices, you are to me like wild flowers which I strew over the feet of my beloved Jesus. I sometimes compare these trifles to the heroic virtues, and that is because their enduring nature demands heroism (*Diary*, 208).

TAKE A BREAK TO LOOK UP TO HEAVEN

Oh, how everything drags man towards the earth! But lively faith maintains the soul in the higher regions and assigns self-love its proper place; that is to say, the lowest one (*Diary*, 210).

I must not let myself become absorbed in the whirl of work, [but] take a break to look up to heaven (*Diary*, 226).

O, you days of work and of monotony, you are not monotonous to me at all, for each moment brings me new graces and opportunity to do good (*Diary*, 245).

$\mathcal{K}$EEPING YOU COMPANY THROUGHOUT THE DAY

I prefer to be a lowly drudge in the convent than a queen in the world (*Diary*, 254).

Jesus, when You come to me in Holy Communion, You who, together with the Father and the Holy Spirit, have deigned to dwell in the little heaven of my heart, I try to keep You company throughout the day. I do not leave You alone for even a moment (*Diary*, 486).

When I am asleep I offer Him every beat of my heart; when I awaken I immerse myself in Him without saying a word (*Diary*, 486).

Adoring And Thanking God Daily

When I awaken I adore the Holy Trinity for a short while and thank God for having deigned to give me yet another day, that the mystery of the incarnation of His Son may once more be repeated in me, and that once again His sorrowful Passion may unfold before my eyes (*Diary*, 486).

I go everywhere with Jesus; His presence accompanies me everywhere (*Diary*, 486).

BATHING DAILY IN THE RAYS OF MERCY

Only love has meaning; it raises up our smallest actions into infinity (*Diary*, 502).

My Jesus, my strength, my peace, my repose; my soul bathes daily in the rays of Your mercy. There is not a moment in my life when I do not experience Your mercy, O God. I count on nothing in my whole life, but only on Your infinite mercy. It is the guiding thread of my life, O Lord, My soul is filled with God's mercy (*Diary*, 697).

I try always to be a Bethany for Jesus, so that He may rest here after all His labors (*Diary*, 735).

J Walk With Lifted Head

Oh, how beautiful is the world of the spirit! And so real that, by comparison, the exterior life is just a vain illusion and powerlessness (*Diary*, 884).

Although the desert is fearful, I walk with lifted head and eyes fixed on the sun; that is to say, on the merciful Heart of Jesus (*Diary*, 886).

The Simplest Tasks With Great Care

A soul in love with God and immersed in Him approaches her duties with the same dispositions as she does Holy Communion and carries out the simplest tasks with great care, under the loving gaze of God (*Diary*, 890).

† I am going forward through life amidst rainbows and storms, but with my head held high with pride, for I am a royal child. I feel that the blood of Jesus is circulating in my veins, and I have put my trust in the great mercy of the Lord (*Diary*, 992).

CHANGING DRABNESS INTO PERSONAL SANCTITY

I feel that I have been totally imbued with God and, with this God, I am going back to my everyday life, so drab, tiresome, and wearying, trusting that He whom I feel in my heart will change this drabness into my personal sanctity (*Diary*, 1363).

Observing myself and those who are close to me, I have come to understand how great an influence I have on other souls, not by any heroic deeds, as these are striking in themselves, but by small actions like a movement of the hand, a look, and many other things too numerous to mention, which have an effect on and reflect in the souls of others, as I myself have noticed (*Diary*, 1475).

Every Moment Of My Life Is Filled

† There are no indifferent moments in my life, since every moment of my life is filled with prayer, suffering, and work. If not in one way, then in another, I glorify God; and if God were to give me a second life, I do not know whether I would make better use of it ... (*Diary*, 1545).

I want to live in the spirit of faith. I accept everything that comes my way as given me by the loving will of God, who sincerely desires my happiness (*Diary*, 1549).

CONSIDERING EACH MOMENT IN LIGHT OF ETERNITY

† Before each important action, I will stop
to consider for a moment what relationship it
has to eternal life and what may be the main
reason for my undertaking it: is it for the glory
of God, or for the good of my own soul, or for
the good of the souls of others? If my heart says
yes, then I will not swerve from carrying out
the given action, unmindful of either obstacles
or sacrifices (*Diary*, 1549).

My Jesus, I now see that I have gone through
all the stages of my life following You:
childhood, youth, vocation, apostolic work,
Tabor, Gethsemane, and now I
am already with You on Calvary
(*Diary*, 1580).

Sin, Sinners

August 11 - 17

Saint Faustina's compassion for sinners was the heart of her life and mission of mercy. She interceded for sinners, offered her sufferings for sinners, and wrote her *Diary* for the sake of sinners. She sought to encourage sinners of God's great mercy. For instance, she wrote, "And fear nothing, dear soul, whoever you are; the greater the sinner, the greater his right to Your mercy, O Lord. O incomprehensible Goodness! God is the first to stoop to the sinner" (*Diary*, 598).

Saint Faustina particularly desired to unite herself with Jesus in making atonement for sinners. She told Jesus, "Transform me into Yourself, O Jesus, that I may be a living sacrifice and pleasing to You. I desire to atone at each moment for poor sinners" (*Diary*, 908).

What about us? In the circumstances of our daily lives, how can we offer our sufferings and trials for sinners?

THE FIRST TO STOOP
TO THE SINNER

✝ O God, You are compassion itself for
the greatest sinners who sincerely repent.
The greater the sinner, the greater his right
to God's mercy (*Diary*, 423).

✝ And fear nothing, dear soul, whoever you
are; the greater the sinner, the greater his right
to Your mercy, O Lord. O incomprehensible
Goodness! God is the first to stoop to the
sinner (*Diary*, 598).

I INCESSANTLY PLEAD GOD'S MERCY FOR SINNERS

How terribly souls suffer there [hell]! Consequently, I pray even more fervently for the conversion of sinners. I incessantly plead God's mercy upon them (*Diary*, 741).

† You are a bottomless sea of mercy for us sinners; and the greater the misery, the more right we have to Your mercy (*Diary*, 793).

Giving Everything Away
For The Sake Of Sinners

My soul is in a sea of suffering. Sinners have taken everything away from me, But that is all right; I have given everything away for their sake that they might know that You are good and infinitely merciful (*Diary*, 893).

† Transform me into Yourself, O Jesus, that I may be a living sacrifice and pleasing to You. I desire to atone at each moment for poor sinners (*Diary*, 908).

OFFERING EVERYTHING FOR SINNERS

Jesus, I offer everything today for sinners. Let the blows of Your justice fall on me, and the sea of Your mercy engulf the poor sinners (*Diary*, 927).

When I see Jesus tormented, my heart is torn to pieces, and I think: what will become of sinners if they do not take advantage of the Passion of Jesus: In His Passion, I see a whole sea of mercy (*Diary*, 948).

SETTING AJAR THE DOOR OF THE HEART

I learned in the depths of my soul how horrible sin was, even the smallest sin, and how much it tormented the soul of Jesus. I would rather suffer a thousand hells than commit even the smallest venial sin (*Diary*, 1016).

† One thing alone is necessary: that the sinner set ajar the door of his heart, be it ever so little, to let in a ray of God's merciful grace, and then God will do the rest (*Diary*, 1507).

The Sins Of The World

† Even if I had had the sins of the whole world, as well as the sins of all the condemned souls weighing on my conscience, I would not have doubted God's goodness but, without hesitation, would have thrown myself into the abyss of The Divine Mercy, which is always open to us; and, with a heart crushed to dust, I would have cast myself at His feet, abandoning myself totally to His holy will, which is mercy itself (*Diary,* 1552).

A light illumined my soul, and I saw the whole abyss of my misery. In that same moment I nestled close to the Most Sacred Heart of Jesus with so much trust that even if I had all the sins of the damned weighing on my conscience, I would have not doubted God's mercy (*Diary,* 1318).

A Holocaust For Sinners On Mercy Sunday

Low Sunday [Mercy Sunday]. Today, I again offered myself to the Lord as a holocaust for sinners. My Jesus, if the end of my life is already approaching, I beg You most humbly, accept my death in union with You as a holocaust which I offer You today, while I still have full possession of my faculties and a fully conscious will (*Diary*, 1680).

[I also offered myself] that sinners, especially dying sinners, may have recourse to Your mercy and experience the unspeakable effects of this mercy (*Diary*, 1680).

Grace

August 18 - September 4

Faithfulness to the grace of God was a major characteristic of the spiritual life of St. Faustina. She wrote clearly about her desire to always cooperate with the grace of God. Saint Faustina desired to do nothing except in faithfulness to the grace of God. Thus, she could write, "I make no movement, no gesture after my own liking, because I am bound by grace; I always consider what is more pleasing to Jesus" (*Diary*, 380).

One important aspect of her reliance on God's grace is that St. Faustina realized she could not trust in her own strength. On one occasion, for instance, she wrote, "I am not counting on my own strength, but on His omnipotence for, as He gave me the grace of knowing His holy will, He will also grant me the grace of fulfilling it" (*Diary*, 615).

How can we cooperate more with God's grace in our own lives? Do we tend to rely too much on our own strength? If so, we can remind ourselves to trust more in God's grace and less on ourselves — perhaps by saying frequently, "Jesus, I trust in You!"

Grace Is Given For Each Hour

The grace which is given me in this hour
will not be repeated in the next. It may be
given me again, but it will not be the same
grace. Time goes on, never to return again.
Whatever is enclosed in it will never change;
it seals with a seal for eternity (*Diary*, 62).

Few are the souls that are always watchful
for divine graces, and even fewer [are the]
souls who follow those inspirations faithfully
(*Diary*, 138).

Every Single Grace Comes Through Prayer

Oh, how wretched my soul is for having wasted so many graces! (*Diary*, 145).

There is no soul which is not bound to pray, for every single grace comes to the soul through prayer (*Diary*, 146).

How can this be; You are God and I — I am Your creature. You, the Immortal King and I, a beggar and misery itself! But now all is clear to me; Your grace and Your love, O Lord, will fill the gulf between You, Jesus, and me (*Diary*, 199).

BEING FAITHFUL TO A PARTICULAR GRACE

Lord, transform me completely into Yourself,
maintain in me a holy zeal for Your glory,
give me the grace and spiritual strength to
do Your holy will in all things (*Diary*, 240).

O, you days of work and of monotony,
you are not monotonous to me at all, for
each moment brings me new graces and
opportunity to do good (*Diary*, 245).

† Now I understand what it means to
be faithful to a particular grace. That one
grace draws down a whole series
of others (*Diary*, 263).

*B*OUND BY GRACE

I do not envy the Seraphim their fire,
for I have a greater gift deposited in my
heart. They admire You in rapture, but
Your Blood mingles with mine (*Diary,* 278).

Let no soul, even the most miserable,
fall prey to doubt; for, as long as one is
alive, each one can become a great saint,
so great is the power of God's grace. It
remains only for us not to oppose God's
action (*Diary,* 283).

I make no movement, no gesture after my
own liking, because I am bound by grace;
I always consider what is more pleasing to
Jesus (*Diary,* 380).

ℱORGIVING RELEASES GRACES

† He who knows how to forgive prepares
for himself many graces from God. As often
as I look upon the Cross, so often will I forgive
with all my heart (*Diary*, 390).

No greater joy is to be found than that
of loving God. Already here on earth we
can taste the happiness of those in heaven by
an intimate union with God, a union that is
extraordinary and often quite incomprehensible
to us. One can attain this very grace through
simple faithfulness of soul (*Diary*, 507).

GRACES INTENDED
FOR OTHER SOULS

The Mother of God told me to do what
she had done, that, even when joyful, I should
always keep my eyes fixed on the Cross, and she
told me that the graces God was granting me
were not for me alone, but for other souls
as well (*Diary*, 561).

God is very displeased with lack of trust in Him,
and this is why some souls lose many graces.
Distrust hurts His most sweet Heart, which
is full of goodness and incomprehensible
love for us (*Diary*, 595).

THE GRACE OF KNOWING GOD'S WILL

I am not counting on my own strength,
but on His omnipotence for, as He gave me
the grace of knowing His holy will, He will also
grant me the grace of fulfilling it (*Diary*, 615).

An extraordinary peace entered my soul
when I reflected on the fact that, despite
great difficulties, I had always faithfully
followed God's will as I knew it. O Jesus,
grant me the grace to put Your will into
practice as I have come to know it,
O God (*Diary*, 666).

ℱIDELITY TO THE TINIEST GRACE

I understood that God's grace must be received just as God sends it, in the way He wants, and one must receive it in that form under which God sends it to us (*Diary*, 715).

† O my Jesus, I am making at this very moment a firm and eternal resolution by virtue of Your grace and mercy, fidelity to the tiniest grace of Yours (*Diary*, 716).

THE GRACE OF LOVING YOU MORE

For my part, I have done everything, and it is now Your turn, my Jesus, and in this way Your cause will be made apparent. I am totally in accord with Your will; do with me as You please, O Lord, but only grant me the grace of loving You more and more ardently (*Diary*, 751).

I have discovered a fountain of happiness in my soul, and it is God. O my God, I see that everything that surrounds me is filled with God, and most of all my own soul, which is adorned with the grace of God (*Diary*, 887).

The Test Of Patience

† Before every major grace, my soul undergoes a test of patience, for I feel the grace, but do not yet possess it. My spirit burns with impatience, but the hour has not yet come (*Diary*, 1084).

If the Lord demands something of a soul, He gives it the means to carry it out, and through grace He makes it capable of doing this (*Diary*, 1090).

*T*HE GRACE OF PRUDENCE

Grace from God was given to me precisely
because I was the weakest of all people;
this is why the Almighty has surrounded
me with His special mercy (*Diary*, 1099).

Virtue without prudence is not virtue at all.
We should often pray to the Holy Spirit
for this grace of prudence (*Diary*, 1106).

Great Graces Often Come With suffering

My sanctity and perfection consist in the close union of my will with the will of God. God never violates our free will. It is up to us whether we want to receive God's grace or not. It is up to us whether we will cooperate with it or waste it (*Diary*, 1107).

Divine light can do more in one moment than I, fatiguing myself for several days (*Diary*, 1250).

God often grants many and great graces out of regard for the souls who are suffering, and He withholds many punishments solely because of the suffering souls (*Diary*, 1268).

Despite All The Graces

My soul is filled with God's light and nourishes itself from Him. My feelings are as if dead. This is a purely spiritual union with God; it is a great predominance of spirit over nature (*Diary*, 1278).

My God, despite all the graces, I long without cease to be eternally united with my God; and the better I know Him, the more ardently I desire Him (*Diary*, 1303).

RADIATE ME WITH YOUR GRACE

I desire to come out of this retreat a saint,
even though human eyes will not notice
this, not even those of the superiors. I abandon
myself entirely to the action of Your grace.
Let Your will be accomplished entirely in me,
O Lord (*Diary,* 1326).

I expose my heart to the action of Your grace
like a crystal exposed to the rays of the sun.
May Your image be reflected in it, O my God,
to the extent that it is possible to be reflected
in the heart of a creature. Let Your divinity
radiate through me, O You who dwell in
my soul (*Diary,* 1336).

A TORRENT OF GRACES

As I was praying before the Blessed Sacrament and greeting the five wounds of Jesus, at each salutation I felt a torrent of graces gushing into my soul, giving me a foretaste of heaven and absolute confidence in God's mercy (*Diary*, 1337).

O Lord, deify my actions so that they will merit eternity; although my weakness is great, I trust in the power of Your grace, which will sustain me *(Diary*, 1371).

Give Me The Grace To Love You

Do not lessen any of my sufferings, only give me strength to bear them. Do with me as You please, Lord, only give me the grace to be able to love You in every event and circumstance. Lord, do not lessen my cup of bitterness, only give me strength that I may be able to drink it all (*Diary*, 1489).

O merciful Lord, it is only out of mercy that You have lavished these gifts upon me. Seeing all these free gifts within me, with deep humility I worship Your incomprehensible goodness (*Diary*, 1523).

*T*HE GREATEST OF ALL GIFTS

Jesus, fortify the powers of my soul that the enemy gain nothing. Without You, I am weakness itself. What am I without Your grace if not an abyss of my own misery? Misery is my possession (*Diary*, 1630).

The greater the graces which my heart receives, the deeper it plunges itself in humility (*Diary*, 1661).

I thanked the Lord Jesus for having deigned to redeem us and for having given us that greatest of all gifts; namely, His love in Holy Communion; that is, His very own Self (*Diary*, 1670).

THE STRENGTH TO ENDURE

O Christ, although much effort is required,
all things can be done with Your grace
(*Diary*, 1696).

My God, although my sufferings are great
and protracted, I accept them from Your hands
as magnificent gifts. I accept them all, even the
ones that other souls have refused to accept.
You can come to me with everything, my Jesus;
I will refuse You nothing. I ask You for only one
thing: give me the strength to endure them
and grant that they may be meritorious.
Here is my whole being; do with me as
You please (*Diary*, 1795).

Blessed
Sacrament,
Eucharist,
Mass

September 5 - 21

*S*he signed her name at the beginning of each of her six notebooks with her full name "Sister Faustina of the Most Blessed Sacrament" (see *Diary*, 2, 523, 1003, 1233, 1590). Each year on New Year's Day, it was the custom for the Sisters to draw a card with their patron for the year written on it. For 1935, Sr. Faustina's card read: "Patron of the Year 1935 — The Most Blessed Eucharist" (*Diary*, 360).

She wrote extensively of her great devotion to the Holy Eucharist. A special gem stands out for me that shows how much she yearned to receive Jesus in Holy Communion: "The most solemn moment of my life is the moment when I receive Holy Communion. I long for each Holy Communion, and for every Holy Communion I give thanks to the Most Holy Trinity" (*Diary*, 1804).

As you read these gems of St. Faustina, ask the Lord to increase your love for Him at Holy Communion and whenever you adore Him in the Most Blessed Sacrament. He yearns to strengthen you and show you the immensity of His love in the Holy Eucharist.

O PRISONER OF LOVE

When I feel that the suffering is more
than I can bear, I take refuge in the Lord
in the Blessed Sacrament, and I speak to
Him with profound silence (*Diary*, 73).

Oh, who will comprehend Your love
and Your unfathomable mercy toward us!
O Prisoner of Love, I lock up my poor heart
in this tabernacle, that it may adore You without
cease night and day (*Diary*, 80).

The Eucharist Gives Courage And Strength

The courage and strength that are in me are not of me, but of Him who lives in me — it is the Eucharist (*Diary*, 91).

O my Jesus, the misunderstandings are so great; sometimes, were it not for the Eucharist, I would not have the courage to go any further along the way You have marked out for me (*Diary*, 91).

Spending My Free Moments In Adoration

This day, my spirit was set aflame with special love for the Eucharist. It seemed to me that I was transformed into a blazing fire (*Diary*, 160).

O Living Host, my one and only strength, fountain of love and mercy, embrace the whole world. … Oh, blessed be the instant and the moment when Jesus left us His most merciful Heart! (*Diary*, 223).

I will spend all my free moments at the feet of [Our Lord in] the Blessed Sacrament. At the feet of Jesus, I will seek light, comfort, and strength (*Diary*, 224).

Most Sweet Eucharistic Heart

I will comfort the most sweet Eucharistic Heart continuously and will play harmonious melodies on the strings of my heart. Suffering is the most harmonious melody of all (*Diary*, 385).

Often during Mass, I see the Lord in my soul; I feel His presence which pervades my being. I sense His divine gaze; I have long talks with Him without saying a word; I know what His divine Heart desires, and I always do what will please Him the most. I love Him to distraction, and I feel that I am being loved by God (*Diary*, 411).

*H*EAL MY TONGUE, LORD

† Jesus, when You come to me in
Holy Communion, You who, together
with the Father and the Holy Spirit, have
deigned to dwell in the little heaven of my
heart, I try to keep You company throughout
the day, I do not leave You alone for even
a moment (*Diary*, 486).

When I receive Holy Communion, I entreat
and beg the Savior to heal my tongue, that I
may never fail in love of neighbor (*Diary*, 590).

*H*IDDEN LIKE A LITTLE WAFER

O Jesus, outwardly I want to be hidden, just
like this little wafer wherein the eye perceives
nothing, and yet I am a host consecrated to
You (*Diary*, 641).

I spend every free moment at the feet of
the hidden God. He is my Master; I ask Him
about everything; I speak to Him about everything.
Here I obtain strength and light; here I learn
everything; here I am given light on how to
act toward my neighbor (*Diary*, 704).

ENCLOSED IN THE TABERNACLE WITH JESUS

I have enclosed myself in the tabernacle together with Jesus, my Master. He Himself drew me into the fire of living love on which everything converges (*Diary*, 704).

It is my delight to spend long hours at the feet of the hidden God, and the hours pass like minutes as I lose track of time (*Diary*, 784).

O Living Bread

† All my strength is in You, O Living Bread.
It would be difficult for me to live through
the day if I did not receive Holy Communion.
It is my shield; without You, Jesus, I know
not how to live (*Diary*, 814).

It is only in eternity that we shall know
the great mystery effected in us by Holy
Communion. O most precious moments
of my life! (*Diary*, 840).

O Blessed Host

A soul in love with God and immersed
in Him approaches her duties with the same
dispositions as she does Holy Communion and
carries out the simplest tasks with great care,
under the loving gaze of God (*Diary,* 890).

O Blessed Host, support me and seal my lips
against all murmuring and complaint. When
I am silent, I know I shall be victorious
(*Diary,* 896).

† Oh, what awesome mysteries take place
during Mass! A great mystery is accomplished
in the Holy Mass (*Diary,* 914).

*H*OLY COMMUNION SUSTAINS ME

One day we will know what God is doing
for us in each Mass, and what sort of gift
He is preparing in it for us (*Diary*, 914).

† One thing alone sustains me, and that
is Holy Communion. From it I draw my
strength; in it is all my comfort. I fear life on
days when I do not receive Holy Communion.
I fear my own self (*Diary*, 1037).

† Jesus concealed in the Host is everything
to me. From the tabernacle I draw strength,
power, courage, and light. Here, I seek
consolation in time of anguish (*Diary*, 1037).

*M*ary Prepares Me For Holy Communion

† I would not know how to give glory to God if I did not have the Eucharist in my heart (*Diary*, 1037).

Before every Holy Communion I earnestly ask the Mother of God to help me prepare my soul for the coming of her Son, and I clearly feel her protection over me. I entreat her to be so gracious as to enkindle in me the fire of God's love, such as burned in her own pure heart at the time of the Incarnation of the Word of God (*Diary*, 1114).

*M*Y HEART IS A LIVING TABERNACLE

† Most sweet Jesus, set on fire my love for You and transform me into Yourself. Divinize me that my deeds may be pleasing to You. May this be accomplished by the power of the Holy Communion which I receive daily. Oh, how greatly I desire to be wholly transformed into You, O Lord! (*Diary*, 1289).

† My heart is a living tabernacle in which the living Host is reserved. I have never sought God in some far-off place, but within myself. It is in the depths of my own being that I commune with my God (*Diary*, 1302).

DIVINE MERCY HIDDEN IN THE BLESSED SACRAMENT

As I was praying before the Blessed Sacrament and greeting the five wounds of Jesus, at each salutation I felt a torrent of graces gushing into my soul, giving me a foretaste of heaven and absolute confidence in God's mercy (*Diary*, 1337).

All the strength of my soul flows from the Blessed Sacrament. I spend all my free moments in conversation with Him. He is my Master (*Diary*, 1404).

† The mercy of God, hidden in the Blessed Sacrament, the voice of the Lord who speaks to us from the throne of mercy:
Come to Me, all of you
(*Diary*, 1485).

The Whole Secret Of My Sanctity

Jesus, there is one more secret in my life, the deepest and dearest to my heart: it is You Yourself when You come to my heart under the appearance of bread. Herein lies the whole secret of my sanctity. Here my heart is so united with Yours as to be but one. There are no more secrets, because all that is Yours is mine, and all that is mine is Yours (*Diary*, 1489).

Now that I have difficulty sleeping at night, because my suffering won't allow it, I visit all the churches and chapels and, if only for a brief moment, I make an act of adoration before the Blessed Sacrament (*Diary*, 1501).

Consecrate Me Yourself

I am a white host before You, O Divine Priest.
Consecrate me Yourself, and may my
[transformation] be known only to You.
I stand before You each day as a sacrificial
host and implore Your mercy upon the
world (*Diary*, 1564).

On leaving the earth, O Lord, You wanted
to stay with us, and so You left us Yourself
in the Sacrament of the Altar, and You opened
wide Your mercy to us. There is no misery that
could exhaust You; You have called us all to this
fountain of love, to this spring of God's
compassion. Here is the tabernacle
of Your mercy, here is the remedy
for all our ills (*Diary*, 1747).

I Long For Each Holy Communion

One day during Holy Mass, the Lord gave me a deeper knowledge of His holiness and His majesty, and at the same time I saw my own misery. This knowledge made me happy, and my soul drowned itself completely in His mercy. I felt enormously happy (*Diary*, 1801).

† The most solemn moment of my life is the moment when I receive Holy Communion. I long for each Holy Communion, and for every Holy Communion I give thanks to the Most Holy Trinity (*Diary*, 1804).

A Fountain Of Mercy

I long for the time when God will come
to my heart. I throw myself in His arms
and tell Him about my inability and my
misery. I pour out all the pain of my heart,
for not being able to love Him as much as
I want. I arouse within myself acts of faith,
hope, and charity and live on that throughout
the day (*Diary*, 1813).

Today, I feel an abyss of misery in my soul.
I want to approach Holy Communion as a
fountain of mercy and to drown myself
completely in this ocean of love (*Diary*, 1817).

Silence,
Solitude

September 22 - 30

As both a mystic and a religious, St. Faustina enjoyed moments of silence and solitude with the Lord. She even goes so far as to say, "My happiest moments are when I am alone with my Lord" (*Diary,* 289).

It was in silence that God Himself would speak to her heart. As she wrote, "Silence is [God's] language, though secret, yet living and powerful" (*Diary,* 888). And it was precisely in solitude that she experienced an inconceivable happiness because she was alone with God. "No one can conceive the happiness which my heart enjoys in its solitude, alone with God" (*Diary,* 1395), she wrote.

In our own busy lives, do we make time for silence and solitude, so we can be alone with the Lord? Or do we let the many distractions of modern life crowd Him out? He wants to speak to our hearts and bring us a joy and happiness the world cannot give.

Recollection In God

When I feel that the suffering is more than
I can bear, I take refuge in the Lord in the
Blessed Sacrament, and I speak to Him with
profound silence (*Diary*, 73).

In order to hear the voice of God, one has
to have silence in one's soul and to keep silence;
not a gloomy silence, but an interior silence;
that is to say, recollection in God (*Diary*, 118).

Jesus Always Found Silence In My Heart

There are attacks when a soul has no time
to think or seek advice; then it must enter
into a life-or-death struggle. Sometimes it
is good to flee for cover in the wound of the
Heart of Jesus, without answering a single
word (*Diary*, 145).

Amidst the greatest din, Jesus always found
silence in my heart, although it sometimes
cost me a lot (*Diary*, 185).

I arm myself with patience and silence,
like a dove that does not complain
and feels no bitterness when
its children are being taken
away from it (*Diary*, 209).

I See The Lord In My Soul

Speak little with people, but a good deal with God (*Diary*, 226).

My happiest moments are when I am alone with my Lord. During these moments I experience the greatness of God and my own misery (*Diary*, 289).

Often during Mass, I see the Lord in my soul; I feel His presence which pervades my being. I sense His divine gaze; I have long talks with Him without saying a word; I know what His divine Heart desires, and I always do what will please Him the most. I love Him to distraction, and I feel that I am being loved by God (*Diary*, 411).

A Sword In The Spiritual Struggle

I feel dislike for all things that the world holds in esteem. With all my soul I desire silence and solitude (*Diary*, 432).

Silence is a sword in the spiritual struggle. A talkative soul will never attain sanctity (*Diary*, 477).

When I am asleep I offer Him every beat of my heart; when I awaken I immerse myself in Him without saying a word (*Diary*, 486).

In the sufferings of soul or body, I try to keep silence, for then my spirit gains the strength that flows from the Passion of Jesus (*Diary*, 487).

*K*NOWING HOW TO KEEP SILENCE

In the midst of all sufferings, both physical
and spiritual, as well as in darkness and
desolation, I will remain silent, like a dove,
and not complain (*Diary*, 504).

The Holy Spirit does not speak to a soul
that is distracted and garrulous. He speaks
by His quiet inspirations to a soul that is
recollected, to a soul that knows how to
keep silence (*Diary*, 552).

My spirit communicates with God without
any word being spoken. I am aware that
He is living in me and I in Him (*Diary*, 560).

Silence Reaches The Throne Of God

My life at present flows on in peaceful awareness of God. My silent soul lives on Him, and this conscious life of God in my soul is for me a source of happiness and strength (*Diary*, 887).

† Silence is so powerful a language that it reaches the throne of the living God. Silence is His language, though secret, yet living and powerful (*Diary*, 888).

*P*ATIENCE, PRAYER, AND SILENCE

O Blessed Host, support me and seal my lips against all murmuring and complaint. When I am silent, I know I shall be victorious (*Diary*, 896).

Patience, prayer, and silence — these are what give strength to the soul (*Diary*, 944).

When great sufferings will cause my nature to tremble, and my physical and spiritual strength will diminish, then will I hide myself deep in the open wound of the Heart of Jesus, silent as a dove, without complaint (*Diary*, 957).

Silence In My Heart

When I see that the burden is beyond my strength, I do not consider or analyze it or probe into it, but I run like a child to the Heart of Jesus and say only one word to Him: "You can do all things." And then I keep silent, because I know that Jesus Himself will intervene in the matter, and as for me, instead of tormenting myself, I use that time to love Him (*Diary*, 1033).

I strive for silence in my heart amidst the greatest sufferings, and I protect myself against all attacks with the shield of Your Name (*Diary*, 1040).

*E*NJOYING SOLITUDE, ALONE WITH GOD

Profound silence engulfs my soul. Not a single cloud hides the sun from me. I lay myself entirely open to its rays, that His love may effect a complete transformation in me. I want to come out of this retreat a saint, and this, in spite of everything; that is to say, in spite of my wretchedness, I want to become a saint, and I trust that God's mercy can make a saint even out of such misery as I am, because I am utterly in good will (*Diary*, 1333).

No one can conceive the happiness which my heart enjoys in its solitude, alone with God (*Diary*, 1395).

Sanctity, Holiness

October 1 - 10

Saint Faustina achieved her great desire to be a saint — not just an ordinary saint, but a great saint! She wanted to be a great saint, so she could be useful to the Church and help save souls. Here is how she expressed it in a precious gem: "I strive for the greatest perfection possible in order to be useful to the Church. Greater by far is my bond to the Church" (*Diary*, 1475).

According to St. Faustina, each saint reflects one of God's virtues in a special way. As a saint, she knew that she was called to spread the message of Divine Mercy.

So she told the Lord, "Let Your mercy, O Jesus, be impressed upon my heart and soul like a seal, and this will be my badge in this and the future life. Glorifying Your mercy is the exclusive task of my life" (*Diary*, 1242).

You and I are also called to holiness in our daily lives. This is the clear teaching of the Church. We are all called to be saints! We can begin by asking God for the desire to become a saint and the grace to grow in holiness in whatever circumstances we find ourselves.

$\mathcal{A}$ Bit Of Good Will

† Let no soul, even the most miserable,
fall prey to doubt; for, as long as one is alive,
each one can become a great saint, so great is
the power of God's grace. It remains only for
us not to oppose God's action (*Diary*, 283).

† O my Jesus, how very easy it is to become
holy; all that is needed is a bit of good will. If
Jesus sees this little bit of good will in the soul,
He hurries to give Himself to the soul, and nothing
can stop Him, neither shortcomings nor falls —
absolutely nothing (*Diary*, 291).

*H*OLY SOULS DO GOD'S WILL

Perfection consists in this close union
with God (*Diary*, 457).

Silence is a sword in the spiritual struggle.
A talkative soul will never attain sanctity
(*Diary*, 477).

[Jesus] told me that the most perfect
and holy soul is the one that does the will
of My Father, but there are not many such,
and that He looks with special love upon
the soul who lives His will (*Diary*, 603).

*D*IVINE MERCY IS PRAISED BY HOLY SOULS

I understood that all striving for perfection
and all sanctity consist in doing God's will.
Perfect fulfillment of God's will is maturity
in sanctity; there is no room for doubt here
(*Diary*, 666).

The mercy of the Lord is praised by the holy
souls in heaven who have themselves experienced
that infinite mercy. What these souls do in heaven,
I already will begin to do here on earth
(*Diary*, 753).

† Oh, there would be many more saintly souls
if there were more experienced
and saintly confessors
(*Diary*, 940).

GREAT LOVE FOR YOU

† My Jesus, I understand well that my perfection consists not in the fact that You command me to carry out these great works of Yours — Oh no! — the soul's greatness does not consist in this, but in great love for You (*Diary*, 984).

† My sanctity and perfection consist in the close union of my will with the will of God. God never violates our free will. It is up to us whether we want to receive God's grace or not. It is up to us whether we will cooperate with it or waste it (*Diary*, 1107).

GLORIFYING YOUR MERCY — MY TASK

† O my Jesus, each of Your saints reflects one of Your virtues; I desire to reflect Your compassionate Heart, full of mercy; I want to glorify it. Let Your mercy, O Jesus, be impressed upon my heart and soul like a seal, and this will be my badge in this and the future life. Glorifying Your mercy is the exclusive task of my life (*Diary*, 1242).

Now I understand why there are so few saints; it is because so few souls are deeply humble (*Diary*, 1306).

I desire to come out of this retreat a saint, even though human eyes will not notice this, not even those of the superiors. I abandon myself entirely to the action of Your grace. Let Your will be accomplished entirely in me, O Lord (*Diary*, 1326).

To Live And Die Like A Holy Soul

Profound silence engulfs my soul. Not a single cloud hides the sun from me. I lay myself entirely open to its rays, that His love may effect a complete transformation in me. I want to come out of this retreat a saint, and this, in spite of everything; that is to say, in spite of my wretchedness, I want to become a saint, and I trust that God's mercy can make a saint even out of such misery as I am, because I am utterly in good will (*Diary*, 1333).

In spite of all my defeats, I want to go on fighting like a holy soul and to comport myself like a holy soul. I will not be discouraged by anything, just as nothing can discourage a soul who is holy. I want to live and die like a holy soul, with my eyes fixed on You, Jesus, stretched out on the Cross, as the model for my actions (*Diary*, 1333).

*T*OTALLY IMBUED WITH GOD

I used to look around me for examples and found nothing which sufficed, and I noticed that my state of holiness seemed to falter. But from now on, my eyes are fixed on You, O Christ, who are for me the best of guides. I am confident that You will bless my efforts (*Diary*, 1333).

I feel that I have been totally imbued with God and, with this God, I am going back to my everyday life, so drab, tiresome and wearying, trusting that He whom I feel in my heart will change this drabness into my personal sanctity (*Diary*, 1363).

Wholly Useful To The Church

† I can be wholly useful to the Church by my personal sanctity, which throbs with life in the whole Church, for we all make up one organism in Jesus. That is why I endeavor to make the soil of my heart bear good fruit (*Diary*, 1364).

† My Jesus, You know that from my earliest years I have wanted to become a great saint; that is to say, I have wanted to love You with a love so great that there would be no soul who has hitherto loved You so (*Diary*, 1372).

*H*OLY COMMUNION — THE SECRET OF MY SANCTITY

I strive for the greatest perfection possible in order to be useful to the Church. Greater by far is my bond to the Church (*Diary,* 1475).

† Jesus, there is one more secret in my life, the deepest and dearest to my heart: it is You Yourself when You come to my heart under the appearance of bread. Herein lies the whole secret of my sanctity. Here my heart is so united with Yours as to be but one. There are no more secrets, because all that is Yours is mine, and all that is mine is Yours (*Diary,* 1489).

God Listens To Holy Souls

I am striving for sanctity, because in this
way I shall be useful to the Church
(*Diary*, 1505).

O my Jesus, I know that, in order to be
useful to souls, one has to strive for the
closest possible union with You, who are
Eternal Love. One word from a soul united
to God effects more good in souls than
eloquent discussions and sermons from
an imperfect soul (*Diary*, 1595).

Happiness, Joy, Delight, Rejoice

October 11 - 22

The Sisters who knew St. Faustina commented freely about her joy in their sworn testimonies for her beatification. In her own writing of the *Diary*, she described the greatest joy: "No greater joy is to be found than that of loving God" (*Diary*, 507).

Saint Faustina found that she was happiest when she was alone with the Lord and aware of His abiding presence in her. With complete sincerity, she could say, "I look for no happiness beyond my own interior where God dwells. I rejoice that God dwells within me" (*Diary*, 454).

Further, this great mystic and lover of God knew the happiness that she experienced through her intimate union with God was but a foretaste of the ineffable joy of heaven. She recorded in her *Diary*, "Already here on earth we can taste the happiness of those in heaven by an intimate union with God, a union that is extraordinary and often quite incomprehensible to us" (*Diary*, 507).

We, too, are called to be happy with God in this life and in the next. What is blocking us from experiencing great happiness in God's presence?

God Dwells Within Me

My happiest moments are when I am alone with my Lord. During these moments I experience the greatness of God and my own misery (*Diary*, 289).

† I look for no happiness beyond my own interior where God dwells. I rejoice that God dwells within me; here I abide with Him unendingly; it is here that my greatest intimacy with Him exists (*Diary*, 454).

*N*o Greater Joy

Oh, what great happiness fills my heart from knowing God and the divine life! It is my desire to share this happiness with all people. I cannot keep this happiness locked in my own heart alone, for His flames burn me and cause my bosom and my entrails to burst asunder (*Diary*, 491).

No greater joy is to be found than that of loving God (*Diary*, 507).

Already here on earth we can taste the happiness of those in heaven by an intimate union with God, a union that is extraordinary and often quite incomprehensible to us. One can attain this very grace through simple faithfulness of soul (*Diary*, 507).

*U*NSURPASSABLE HAPPINESS

If there is a truly happy soul upon earth,
it can only be a truly humble soul (*Diary*, 593).

A humble soul does not trust itself, but places
all its confidence in God. God defends the humble
soul and lets Himself into its secrets, and the soul
abides in unsurpassable happiness which no one
can comprehend (*Diary*, 593).

Happy is the soul that calls upon the
mercy of the Lord (*Diary*, 598).

My goal is God ... and my happiness is
in accomplishing His will, and nothing in
the world can disturb this
happiness for me: no power,
no force of any kind
(*Diary*, 775).

*R*EJOICING IN HIM

I have discovered a fountain of happiness
in my soul, and it is God. O my God, I see
that everything that surrounds me is filled
with God, and most of all my own soul, which
is adorned with the grace of God (*Diary*, 887).

I am coming to know God's greatness more
and more and to rejoice in Him. I remain
unceasingly with Him in the depths of my
heart. It is in my own soul that I most easily
find God (*Diary*, 903).

A Joy That I Cannot Contain

† Oh, if only the suffering soul knew how it is loved by God, it would die of joy and excess of happiness! Some day, we will know the value of suffering, but then we will no longer be able to suffer. The present moment is ours (*Diary,* 963.)

I often receive light and the knowledge of the interior life of God and of God's intimate disposition, and this fills me with unutterable trust and a joy that I cannot contain within myself; I desire to dissolve completely in Him ... (*Diary,* 1102).

I Am Pleasing To Him

† I do not know how to live without God,
but I also feel that God, absolutely self-sufficient
though He is, cannot be happy without me ...
(*Diary*, 1120).

There is no greater happiness than when
God gives me to know interiorly that every
beat of my heart is pleasing to Him, and when
He shows me that He loves me in a special way
(*Diary*, 1121).

What happiness it is to have the consciousness
of God in one's heart and to live in close intimacy
with Him (*Diary*, 1135).

Oh, How Happy I Am!

God's greatness does not frighten me,
but makes me happy. By giving Him glory,
I myself am lifted up. On seeing His happiness,
I myself am made happy, because all that is
in Him flows back upon me (*Diary*, 1246).

All the good that is in me is due to Holy
Communion. I owe everything to it. I feel
that this holy fire has transformed me completely.
Oh, how happy I am to be a dwelling place for
You, O Lord! My heart is a temple in which
You dwell continually ... (*Diary*, 1392).

I Rejoice That You Are So Powerful

† No one can conceive the happiness which my heart enjoys in its solitude, alone with God (*Diary*, 1395).

O my Lord, my soul is the most wretched of all, and yet You stoop to it with such kindness! I see clearly Your greatness and my littleness, and therefore I rejoice that You are so powerful and without limit, and so I rejoice greatly at being so little (*Diary*, 1417).

Oh, how great is the mercy of God, who allows man to participate in such a high degree in His divine happiness! At the same time, what great pain pierces my heart [at the thought] that so many souls have spurned this happiness (*Diary*, 1439).

*M*Y HEART DISSOLVES IN JOY

† O incomprehensible God, my heart dissolves in joy that You have allowed me to penetrate the mysteries of Your mercy! Everything begins with Your mercy and ends with Your mercy (*Diary*, 1506).

Everlasting love, pure flame, burn in my heart ceaselessly and deify my whole being, according to Your infinite pleasure by which You summoned me into existence and called me to take part in Your everlasting happiness (*Diary*, 1523).

The Happiness Of Other Souls

I want to live in the spirit of faith. I accept everything that comes my way as given me by the loving will of God, who sincerely desires my happiness (*Diary*, 1549).

The happiness of other souls fills me with a new joy, and when I see the higher gifts in some soul, my heart soars up to the Lord in a new hymn of adoration (*Diary*, 1671).

THE DELIGHT OF MY HEART

To converse with You, O Lord, is the delight
of my heart. In You I find everything that
my heart could desire (*Diary*, 1692).

As I was meditating on the blessings of God,
my heart was burning with a love so strong
that it seemed my breast would burst
(*Diary*, 1705).

I FELT ENORMOUSLY HAPPY

The moments which are most pleasant to me are those when I converse with the Lord within the center of my being. I try my very best not to leave Him alone. He likes to be always with us ... (*Diary*, 1793).

One day during Holy Mass, the Lord gave me a deeper knowledge of His holiness and His majesty, and at the same time I saw my own misery. This knowledge made me happy, and my soul drowned itself completely in His mercy. I felt enormously happy (*Diary*, 1801).

Presence of God

October 23 - 24

The experience of God's presence was a fundamental characteristic of St. Faustina's life. It was an expression of her intimate union with the Lord. She experienced the Lord's Eucharistic presence in a such a continuous way that she could say: "I have come to know that Holy Communion remains in me until the next Holy Communion. A vivid and clearly felt presence of God continues in my soul" (*Diary*, 1302).

Saint Faustina even goes so far as to talk of the Lord as her "constant companion," saying, "He is present to me at every moment" (*Diary*, 318).

Consider how you can be more conscious of God's presence in your daily life. It might be as simple as conversing with Him in your heart as you go about your day — the way a small child would with a parent.

$\mathcal{P}$RESENT AT EVERY MOMENT

I am never alone, because He is my constant
companion. He is present to me at every moment.
Our intimacy is very close, through a union of
blood and of life (*Diary*, 318).

Often during Mass, I see the Lord in my soul;
I feel His presence which pervades my being.
I sense His divine gaze; I have long talks with
Him without saying a word; I know what His
divine Heart desires, and I always do what will
please Him the most. I love Him to distraction,
and I feel that I am being loved by God
(*Diary*, 411).

*F*EELING GOD'S PRESENCE PHYSICALLY

My spirit is so pervaded with God that I feel it physically, and the body partakes of these joys (*Diary*, 582).

God's presence pervades my soul, not only in a spiritual way, but I feel it in a physical way also (*Diary*, 747).

When it happens that the living presence of God, which [a soul] enjoys almost constantly, leaves her, she then tries to continue living in lively faith. Her soul understands that there are periods of rest and periods of battle (*Diary*, 890).

Thanksgiving

October 25 - 29

*W*hen St. Faustina combined her trust in Jesus with thanksgiving, the combination was dynamite: TNT! (Tri Nitro Toluene). By trust and thanksgiving, she would overcome her sense of her misery. Thanksgiving was a major way in which she praised and glorified the Merciful Savior for His great mercy toward us.

What really helped St. Faustina to grow in having a thankful heart was her realization that she could thank Him for everything because of her complete trust in Him. In all honesty, she was able to say, "I do not prefer consolations over bitterness or bitterness over consolations, but thank You, O Jesus, for everything!" (*Diary*, 343). Now that's trust in action!

We, too, are called to cultivate a spirit of thanksgiving in our lives, even when we encounter difficulties and trials.

*H*is Great Mercy Towards Me

I will show my gratitude unceasingly to
God for His great mercy towards me
(*Diary*, 224).

Thank You, Jesus, for the great favor
of making known to me the whole abyss
of my misery. I know that I am an abyss of
nothingness and that, if Your holy grace did
not hold me up, I would return to nothingness
in a moment. And so, with every beat of my
heart, I thank You, my God, for Your great
mercy towards me (*Diary*, 256).

THANKING GOD FOR EVERYTHING

† I do not prefer consolations over bitterness or bitterness over consolations, but thank You, O Jesus, for everything! (*Diary*, 343).

When I awaken I adore the Holy Trinity for a short while and thank God for having deigned to give me yet another day, that the mystery of the incarnation of His Son may once more be repeated in me, and that once again His sorrowful Passion may unfold before my eyes (*Diary*, 486).

Thanks For The Majesty Of God

Thank You, Jesus, for everything, because
it is not the greatness of the works, but the
greatness of the effort that will be rewarded.
What is done out of love is not small,
O my Jesus, for Your eyes see everything
(*Diary*, 1310).

† I want to plunge myself in thanksgiving
before the Majesty of God and to continue
in this prayer of thanksgiving for seven days
and seven nights; and although I will outwardly
carry out all my duties, my spirit will nonetheless
stand continually before the Lord, and all my
exercises will be imbued with
the spirit of thanksgiving
(*Diary*, 1367).

One Single Flame Of Gratitude

† I shall steep myself in a prayer of thanksgiving.
In this way I want to repay, at least in some
small way, for the immensity of God's
blessings (*Diary*, 1367).

My soul became thoroughly immersed in
God, and there issued from my whole being
but one single flame of gratitude and
thanksgiving to God (*Diary*, 1369).

*T*HE GIFT OF HIS VERY OWN SELF

† Thank You in advance, O Lord, for everything Your goodness will send me. Thank You for the cup of suffering from which I shall daily drink. Do not diminish its bitterness, O Lord, but strengthen my lips that, while drinking of this bitterness, they may know how to smile for love of You, my Master (*Diary*, 1449).

I thanked the Lord Jesus for having deigned to redeem us and for having given us that greatest of all gifts; namely, His love in Holy Communion; that is, His very own Self (*Diary*, 1670).

Holy Confession

October 30 - 31

Jesus described the Sacrament of Reconciliation or Penance as "the Tribunal of Mercy" in His revelations to St. Faustina. It is one of the great Sacraments of Mercy. Our Lord told St. Faustina that when souls come to confession what they are to reveal is their *misery* and they will receive the *greatest miracles of mercy*: **"Tell souls where they are to look for solace; that is, in the Tribunal of Mercy. There the greatest miracles take place [and] are incessantly repeated,"** He told her. **"To avail oneself of this miracle, it is not necessary to go on a great pilgrimage or to carry out some external ceremony; it suffices to come with faith to the feet of My representative and to reveal to him one's misery. ... The miracle of Divine Mercy restores that soul in full"** (*Diary*, 1448).

As St. Faustina prepared for confession, she would "call to mind the Passion of Jesus" to arouse her "heart to contrition" (*Diary*, 225). She also came to realize that it was important to pray for her confessor "that he might obtain the light of the Holy Spirit" (*Diary*, 647).

Let's learn from St. Faustina how we can better prepare for the Sacrament of Reconciliation. We can start by owning our sins as our misery, which can only be healed by God's mercy. Jesus told St. Faustina — as He tells each of us — **"Give Me your misery, because it is your exclusive property"** (*Diary*, 1318).

CALLING TO MIND THE PASSION

As regards Holy Confession, I shall choose
what costs and humiliates me most. Sometimes
a trifle costs more than something greater
(*Diary*, 225).

I will call to mind the Passion of Jesus
at each confession, to arouse my heart
to contrition (*Diary*, 225).

Healing Through Confession

† We should derive two kinds of profit from Holy Confession:

1. We come to confession to be healed;
2. We come to be educated — like a small child, our soul has constant need of education (*Diary*, 377).

I came to understand one thing: that I must pray much for each of my confessors, that he might obtain the light of the Holy Spirit (*Diary*, 647).

Cross,
Wounds,
Passion

November 1 - 7

Among the greatest of St. Faustina's gems are those on the Passion and the wounds of Jesus. In one vision of the crucified Lord Jesus, she even records, "Precious pearls and diamonds were pouring forth from the wounds in His Heart. I saw how a multitude of souls was gathering these gifts" (*Diary*, 1687).

The Lord Jesus Himself revealed to St. Faustina the immense value in meditating on His Passion. He told her, **"There is more merit to one hour of meditation on My sorrowful Passion than there is to a whole year of flagellation that draws blood; the contemplation of My painful wounds is of great profit to you, and it brings Me great joy"** (*Diary*, 369).

Saint Faustina understood that Jesus' sacrifice was "all-powerful," and she was constantly seeking to join her sacrifices to His. She recorded, "My sacrifice is nothing in itself, but when I join it to the sacrifice of Jesus Christ, it becomes all-powerful and has the power to appease divine wrath" (*Diary*, 482).

The most important way that we can enter into the reality of the Lord's Passion is by participating at Holy Mass as frequently as possible. Further, we can meditate on the Lord's Passion by making the Stations of the Cross. This is especially salutary at 3 p.m., the Hour of Great Mercy, when Jesus died on the Cross (see *Diary*, 1572).

Gaze Upon His Sacred Wounds

In difficult moments I must take refuge
in the wounds of Jesus; I must seek consolation,
comfort, light, and affirmation in the wounds
of Jesus (*Diary*, 226).

I fixed my gaze upon His sacred wounds
and felt happy to suffer with Him. I suffered,
and yet I did not suffer, because I felt happy to
know the depth of His love, and the hour
passed like a minute (*Diary*, 252).

He who wants to learn true humility should
reflect upon the Passion of Jesus (*Diary*, 267).

JOINED TO THE SACRIFICE OF JESUS

Love must be reciprocal. If Jesus tasted
the fullness of bitterness for me, then I,
His bride, will accept all bitterness as
proof of my love for Him (*Diary*, 389).

O Jesus! I sense keenly how Your divine
Blood is circulating in my heart; I have not
the least doubt that Your most pure love has
entered my heart with Your most sacred
Blood (*Diary*, 478).

My sacrifice is nothing in itself, but when
I join it to the sacrifice of Jesus Christ, it
becomes all-powerful and has the power to
appease divine wrath. God loves
us in His Son; the painful
Passion of the Son of God
constantly turns aside the
wrath of God (*Diary*, 482).

The Emptying Of Myself

My name is host — or sacrifice, not in words but in deeds, in the emptying of myself and in becoming like You on the Cross, O good Jesus, my Master! (*Diary*, 485).

When I awaken I adore the Holy Trinity for a short while and thank God for having deigned to give me yet another day, that the mystery of the incarnation of His Son may once more be repeated in me, and that once again His sorrowful Passion may unfold before my eyes (*Diary*, 486).

In the sufferings of soul or body, I try to keep silence, for then my spirit gains the strength that flows from the Passion of Jesus (*Diary*, 487).

A Whole Sea Of Mercy

The Mother of God told me to do what she had done, that, even when joyful, I should always keep my eyes fixed on the Cross, and she told me that the graces God was granting me were not for me alone, but for other souls as well (*Diary*, 561).

When I see Jesus tormented, my heart is torn to pieces, and I think: what will become of sinners if they do not take advantage of the Passion of Jesus: In His Passion, I see a whole sea of mercy (*Diary*, 948).

GREETING THE FIVE WOUNDS OF JESUS

I am going forward through life amidst rainbows and storms, but with my head held high with pride, for I am a royal child. I feel that the Blood of Jesus is circulating in my veins, and I have put my trust in the great mercy of the Lord (*Diary*, 992).

As I was praying before the Blessed Sacrament and greeting the five wounds of Jesus, at each salutation I felt a torrent of graces gushing into my soul, giving me a foretaste of heaven and absolute confidence in God's mercy (*Diary*, 1337).

CLOSE TO THE SUFFERING SOUL

It is You, Jesus, stretched out on the Cross,
who give me strength and are always close
to the suffering soul (*Diary,* 1508).

O my Jesus, my Master, I unite my desires
to the desires that You had on the Cross:
I desire to fulfill Your holy will; I desire the
conversion of souls; I desire that Your mercy
be adored; I desire that the triumph of the
Church be hastened. (*Diary,* 1581)

Gems Pouring Forth From The Wound

I cannot practice any greater mortifications, because I am so very weak. This long illness has sapped my strength completely. I am uniting myself with Jesus through suffering. When I meditate on His Painful Passion, my physical sufferings are lessened (*Diary*, 1625).

Today I saw the Crucified Lord Jesus. Precious pearls and diamonds were pouring forth from the wound in His Heart. I saw how a multitude of souls was gathering these gifts (*Diary*, 1687).

Glory, Glorify

November 8 - 17

One of St. Faustina's gems that especially sparkles is: "Glorifying Your mercy is the exclusive task of my life" (*Diary*, 1242). Saint Faustina wanted to glorify God's mercy in everything she did: in reflecting the compassionate Heart of Jesus, full of mercy; in praising and thanking Him; in proclaiming the Lord's mercy by her works, by her prayers by her deeds, and by her holiness of life.

In understanding more about God's glory, St. Faustina came to realize that "the person who resembles the suffering Jesus here on earth" "will resemble Jesus in His glory" (*Diary*, 604). "She truly sought to live this to the fullest. As she recorded, "I will glorify [Jesus] in abandonment and darkness, in agony and fear, in pain and bitterness, in anguish of spirit and grief of heart" (*Diary*, 1662).

We, too, are called to glorify and praise God in the midst of our sufferings. As we do, the Lord holds out the promise of us sharing in His glory in heaven. There, we will experience glory beyond our understanding.

A Holy Zeal For Your Glory

Lord, transform me completely into Yourself,
maintain in me a holy zeal for Your glory,
give me the grace and spiritual strength to
do Your holy will in all things (*Diary,* 240).

In spite of my great misery I fear nothing,
but hope to sing You a hymn of glory
for ever (*Diary,* 283).

† O Jesus, I wish to glorify Your mercy on
behalf of thousands of souls (*Diary,* 598).

*U*NIMAGINABLE GLORY

† The Lord also gave me to understand what unimaginable glory awaits the person who resembles the suffering Jesus here on earth. That person will resemble Jesus in His glory (*Diary*, 604).

O God, You who pervade my soul, You know that I desire nothing but Your glory (*Diary*, 650).

My Destiny — To Glorify God's Mercy

† I recognized the purpose and destiny
of my life. My purpose is to become closely
united to God through love, and my destiny
is to praise and glorify God's mercy (*Diary*, 729).

I want every soul to glorify the mercy of God,
for each one experiences the effects of that
mercy on himself. The Saints in heaven worship
the mercy of the Lord. I want to worship it even
now, here on earth, and to spread devotion to it in
the way that God demands of me (*Diary*, 745).

Glorify Mercy For Endless Ages

O eternal God, how ardently I desire to glorify this greatest of Your attributes; namely, Your unfathomable mercy (*Diary*, 835).

† I take into my hands the two rays that spring from Your merciful Heart; that is, the Blood and the Water; and I scatter them all over the globe so that each soul may receive Your mercy and, having received it, may glorify it for endless ages (*Diary*, 836).

THE GLORY OF YOUR NAME

O human souls, where are you going to hide on the day of God's anger: Take refuge now in the fount of God's mercy. O what a great multitude of souls I see! They worshiped The Divine Mercy and will be singing the hymn of praise for all eternity (*Diary*, 848).

Oh, how ardently I desire that all mankind turn with trust to Your mercy. Then, seeing the glory of Your Name, my heart will be comforted (*Diary*, 929).

GLORY AND PRAISE TO THE DIVINE MERCY

The soul gives the greatest glory to its
Creator when it turns with trust to
The Divine Mercy (*Diary*, 930).

Let the glory and praise to The Divine Mercy
rise from every creature throughout all ages
and times (*Diary*, 1005).

† O Jesus, I want to live in the present moment,
to live as if this were the last day of my life.
I want to use every moment scrupulously for
the greater glory of God, to use every circumstance
for the benefit of my soul. I want to look upon
everything, from the point of view that nothing
happens without the will of God (*Diary*, 1183).

THE EXCLUSIVE TASK OF MY LIFE

† O my Jesus, each of Your saints reflects
one of Your virtues; I desire to reflect Your
compassionate Heart, full of mercy; I want
to glorify it. Let Your mercy, O Jesus, be
impressed upon my heart and soul like a seal,
and this will be my badge in this and the future
life. Glorifying Your mercy is the exclusive task
of my life (*Diary*, 1242).

† God's greatness does not frighten me, but
makes me happy. By giving Him glory, I myself
am lifted up. On seeing His happiness, I myself
am made happy, because all that is in Him flows
back upon me (*Diary*, 1246).

Giving God The Glory

There are no indifferent moments in my life, since every moment of my life is filled with prayer, suffering, and work. If not in one way, then in another, I glorify God; and if God were to give me a second life, I do not know whether I would make better use of it (*Diary*, 1545).

I know that I will give God the glory He expects of me if I try faithfully to cooperate with God's grace (*Diary*, 1548).

Seeing The Glory Of God's Mercy

In order to write anything at all, I must make use of words, though they cannot render all of what my soul enjoyed on seeing the glory of God's mercy (*Diary*, 1659).

The glory of The Divine Mercy is resounding, even now, in spite of the efforts of its enemies and of Satan himself, who has a great hatred for God's mercy (*Diary*, 1659).

I will glorify [Jesus] in abandonment and darkness, in agony and fear, in pain and bitterness, in anguish of spirit and grief of heart (*Diary*, 1662).

Your Praise And Glory Resound

O Christ, I am most delighted when I see that You are loved, and that Your praise and glory resound, especially the praise of Your mercy. O Christ, to the last moment of my life, I will not stop glorifying Your goodness and mercy. With every drop of my blood, with every beat of my heart, I glorify Your mercy. I long to be entirely transformed into a hymn of Your glory (*Diary*, 1708).

May Your mercy be glorified, O Lord; we will praise it for endless ages. And the angels were amazed at the greatness of the mercy which You have shown for mankind ... (*Diary*, 1743).

Blessed Virgin Mary

November 18 - 20

In a special way, the Blessed Virgin Mary desired to be a mother to St. Faustina, Mary sought to form in St. Faustina, her daughter, her own most characteristic virtues of humility, purity, and love of God. On the Solemnity of the Immaculate Conception in 1937, Our Lady told St. Faustina of her desire for this special relationship: *"My daughter, at God's command I am to be, in a special and exclusive way your Mother; but I desire that you too, in a special way, be my child"* (*Diary*, 1414).

When Our Lady also told St. Faustina to "practice the three virtues that are dearest to me" (humility, purity, and love of God), the saint recorded, "My heart became so wonderfully attracted to these virtues; and I practice them faithfully. They are as though engraved in my heart" (*Diary*, 1415). Thus, St. Faustina could say, "Mary is my Instructress, who is ever teaching me how to live for God" (*Diary*, 620).

Like St. Faustina, we are spiritual children of Mary. Let us seek to imitate her virtues. Most of all, let us ask her to lead us to her Son, Jesus.

*M*Y DEAREST MOTHER

O Mary, my dearest Mother, guide my spiritual life in such a way that it will please your Son (*Diary*, 240).

† The Mother of God told me to do what she had done, that, even when joyful, I should always keep my eyes fixed on the Cross, and she told me that the graces God was granting me were not for me alone, but for other souls as well (*Diary*, 561).

CLOSE TO THE IMMACULATE HEART

† Mary is my Instructress, who is ever teaching me how to live for God (*Diary*, 620).

† The more I imitate the Mother of God, the more deeply I get to know God (*Diary*, 843).

I have been living under the virginal cloak of the Mother of God. She has been guarding me and instructing me. I am quite at peace, close to her Immaculate Heart. Because I am so weak and inexperienced, I nestle like a little child close to her heart (*Diary*, 1097).

*M*ary Helps Me Prepare To Receive Jesus

† Before every Holy Communion I earnestly
ask the Mother of God to help me prepare
my soul for the coming of her Son, and I
clearly feel her protection over me. I entreat
her to be so gracious as to enkindle in me
the fire of God's love, such as burned in
her own pure heart at the time of the
Incarnation of the Word of God
(*Diary*, 1114).

You have indeed prepared a tabernacle for
Yourself: the Blessed Virgin. Her Immaculate
Womb is Your dwelling place, and the inconceivable
miracle of Your mercy takes
place, O Lord. The Word
becomes flesh; God dwells
among us, the Word of God,
Mercy Incarnate (*Diary*, 1745).

The Present Moment

November 21 - 22

For St. Faustina not only was the presence of God real and deeply felt, but the present moment was also precious to her. She recognized, with great insight, that all she really had in accomplishing her mission was the present moment. She wrote, "The past does not belong to me; the future is not mine; with all my soul I try to make use of the present moment" (*Diary*, 351).

A key to St. Faustina living in the present moment was her "unwavering trust" in the Lord. "I live from one hour to the next and am not able to get along in any other way. I want to make the best possible use of the present moment," she said, "faithfully accomplishing everything that it gives me. In all things, I depend on God with unwavering trust" (*Diary*, 1400).

All of us are called to live for God in the present moment. With God's grace, let us break free of the chains of the past and not worry about the future. With all our souls, let us try to make use of the present moment.

*M*AKE USE OF THE PRESENT MOMENT

The past does not belong to me; the future is not mine; with all my soul I try to make use of the present moment (*Diary*, 351).

† O Jesus, I want to live in the present moment, to live as if this were the last day of my life. I want to use every moment scrupulously for the greater glory of God, to use every circumstance for the benefit of my soul. I want to look upon everything, from the point of view that nothing happens without the will of God (*Diary*, 1183).

May You be blessed, O God, for everything You send me. Nothing under the sun happens without Your will. I cannot penetrate Your secrets with regard to myself, but I press my lips to the chalice You offer me (*Diary*, 1208).

✟ROM ONE HOUR TO THE NEXT

† I live from one hour to the next and am not able to get along in any other way. I want to make the best possible use of the present moment, faithfully accomplishing everything that it gives me. In all things, I depend on God with unwavering trust (*Diary*, 1400).

There are no indifferent moments in my life, since every moment of my life is filled with prayer, suffering, and work. If not in one way, then in another, I glorify God; and if God were to give me a second life, I do not know whether I would make better use of it ... (*Diary*, 1545).

Deify,
Divinize,
Transform

November 23 - 30

Saint Faustina desired with all her heart to be transformed into a living presence of Jesus — a presence of His mercy. She used various terms to describe her desire to be transformed, such as divinize me, deify me, and even transconsecrate me. This great mystic was trying to understand and express the mystery of God's love transforming her very being, as she gave herself completely to Him.

In seeking such divinization, St. Faustina's goal was to help Jesus save souls and spread His message of mercy. She told the Merciful Savior, "I want to be completely transformed into Your mercy and to be Your living reflection, O Lord" (*Diary*, 163). In another passage, she said, "I want to be transformed into Jesus in order to be able to give myself completely to souls" (*Diary*, 193).

Jesus wants to transform each of us as well, so we can fulfill our own vocation and state of life. Let's pray with St. Faustina, "My Jesus, penetrate me through and through so that I might be able to reflect You in my whole life" (*Diary*, 1242).

The Totality Of His Delight

At that moment I felt transconsecrated.
My earthly body was the same, but my soul
was different; God was now living in it with
the totality of His delight. This is not a feeling,
but a conscious reality that nothing can obscure
(*Diary*, 137).

I want to be completely transformed into
Your mercy and to be Your living reflection,
O Lord (*Diary*, 163).

O my Jesus, transform me into Yourself,
for You can do all things (*Diary*, 163).

*M*AKE MY HEART
LIKE UNTO YOURS

I want to be transformed into Jesus in
order to be able to give myself completely
to souls (*Diary*, 193).

Lord, transform me completely into Yourself,
maintain in me a holy zeal for Your glory,
give me the grace and spiritual strength to
do Your holy will in all things (*Diary*, 240).

Jesus, make my heart like unto Yours,
or rather transform it into Your own Heart
that I may sense the needs of other hearts,
especially those who are sad and suffering.
May the rays of mercy rest in
my heart (*Diary*, 514).

TRANSFORM ME INTO YOURSELF

O Jesus, my Lord, help me. Let what You
have planned before all ages happen to me.
I am ready at each beckoning of Your holy will.
Enlighten my mind that I may know Your will.
O God, You who pervade my soul, You know
that I desire nothing but Your glory (*Diary*, 650).

O my Jesus, transform me into Yourself by
the power of Your love, that I may be a worthy
tool in proclaiming Your mercy (*Diary*, 783).

Transform me into Yourself and make me
capable of doing Your holy will in all things
and of returning Your love (*Diary*, 832).

A LIVING SACRIFICE

Love is a mystery that transforms everything
it touches into things beautiful and pleasing
to God (*Diary*, 890).

Transform me into Yourself, O Jesus, that
I may be a living sacrifice and pleasing to You.
I desire to atone at each moment for poor
sinners (*Diary*, 908).

I feel that I am being completely transformed
into prayer in order to beg God's mercy for every
soul. O my Jesus, I am receiving You into my heart
as a pledge of mercy for souls (*Diary*, 996).

*D*IVINIZE ME

† My Jesus, penetrate me through and through so that I might be able to reflect You in my whole life. Divinize me so that my deeds may have supernatural value. Grant that I may have love, compassion, and mercy for every soul without exception (*Diary*, 1242).

† Most sweet Jesus, set on fire my love for You and transform me into Yourself. Divinize me that my deeds may be pleasing to You. May this be accomplished by the power of the Holy Communion which I receive daily. Oh, how greatly I desire to be wholly transformed into You, O Lord! (*Diary*, 1289).

$\mathcal{M}$Y HEART IS A TEMPLE FOR YOU

O Lord, deify my actions so that they will merit eternity; although my weakness is great, I trust in the power of Your grace, which will sustain me (*Diary,* 1371.)

† All the good that is in me is due to Holy Communion. I owe everything to it. I feel that this holy fire has transformed me completely. Oh, how happy I am to be a dwelling place for You, O Lord! My heart is a temple in which You dwell continually ... (*Diary,*1392).

Deify My Whole Being

I am being transformed into a flame of love towards You, my God (*Diary*, 1456).

Everlasting love, pure flame, burn in my heart ceaselessly and deify my whole being, according to Your infinite pleasure by which You summoned me into existence and called me to take part in Your everlasting happiness (*Diary*, 1523).

TRANSFORMED, WHOLE AND ENTIRE

O Christ, to the last moment of my life,
I will not stop glorifying Your goodness
and mercy. With every drop of my blood,
with every beat of my heart, I glorify
Your mercy. I long to be entirely
transformed into a hymn of
Your glory (*Diary,* 1708).

† Today, I want to be transformed,
whole and entire, into the love of Jesus
and to offer myself, together with Him,
to the Heavenly Father (*Diary,* 1820).

Merciful Heart of Jesus

December 1 - 11

Jesus has one Heart, and it is both Sacred and Merciful. Hence the Sacred Heart devotion given to St. Margaret Mary Alacoque and The Divine Mercy devotion given to St. Faustina actually complement each other.

In the case of St. Faustina, she repeatedly described how she would flee to the Merciful Heart of Jesus for refuge, like a trusting child, in the midst of attacks and danger. The Merciful Heart of Jesus was her favorite hiding place. On one occasion, she wrote, "O my Savior, conceal me completely in the depths of Your Heart and shield me with Your rays against everything that is not You" (*Diary*, 465).

Saint Faustina also asked Jesus to make her own heart like His own, so she would be equipped to share His love and mercy with others. "My Jesus, make my heart like unto Your merciful Heart," she wrote. "Jesus, help me to go through life doing good to everyone" (*Diary*, 692).

Let's seek refuge in the Merciful Heart of Jesus. And let's join the great Apostle of Divine Mercy in asking, "O Jesus, make my heart like unto Your merciful Heart. Jesus, help me to go through life doing good to everyone" (*Diary*, 692).

THE WOUND OF THE HEART OF JESUS

There are attacks when a soul has no time to think or seek advice; then it must enter into a life-or-death struggle. Sometimes it is good to flee for cover in the wound of the Heart of Jesus, without answering a single word (*Diary*, 145).

With the trust and simplicity of a small child, I give myself to You today, O Lord Jesus, my Master. I leave You complete freedom in directing my soul. Guide me along the paths You wish. I won't question them. I will follow You trustingly. Your merciful Heart can do all things! (*Diary*, 228).

The Most Sweet Eucharistic Heart

Today I place my heart on the paten where
Your Heart has been placed, O Jesus, and
today I offer myself together with You to
God, Your Father and mine, as a sacrifice
of love and praise. Father of Mercy, look
upon the sacrifice of my heart, but through
the wound in the Heart of Jesus (*Diary*, 239).

I will comfort the most sweet Eucharistic
Heart continuously and will play harmonious
melodies on the strings of my heart. Suffering
is the most harmonious melody of all (*Diary*, 385).

In The Depths Of Your Heart

Often during Mass, I see the Lord in my soul;
I feel His presence which pervades my being.
I sense His divine gaze; I have long talks with
Him without saying a word; I know what
His divine Heart desires, and I always do
what will please Him the most. I love
Him to distraction, and I feel that I am
being loved by God (*Diary,* 411).

O my Savior, conceal me completely
in the depths of Your Heart and shield
me with Your rays against everything that
is not You. I beg You, Jesus, let the two rays
that have issued from Your most merciful
Heart continuously nourish my soul
(*Diary,* 465).

*R*AYS OF MERCY IN MY HEART

Jesus, make my heart like unto Yours,
or rather transform it into Your own Heart
that I may sense the needs of other hearts,
especially those who are sad and suffering.
May the rays of mercy rest in my heart
(*Diary,* 514).

God is very displeased with lack of trust
in Him, and this is why some souls lose
many graces. Distrust hurts His most sweet
Heart, which is full of goodness and
incomprehensible love for us (*Diary,* 595).

YOUR MERCIFUL HEART

Do with me as You please; only give me
Your merciful Heart and that is enough
for me (*Diary*, 650).

My Jesus, make my heart like unto
Your merciful Heart. Jesus, help me to
go through life doing good to everyone
(*Diary*, 692).

I must always have a heart which is open
to receive the sufferings of others, and drown
my own sufferings in the Divine Heart so that
they would not be noticed on the outside,
in so far as possible (*Diary*, 792).

THE HEART OF MY SPOUSE

My spirit was immersed in Him as in its
only treasure. My heart rested a while near
the Heart of my Spouse (*Diary*, 801).

O most sweet Jesus who, in Your incomprehensible
kindness, have deigned to unite my wretched heart
to Your most merciful Heart, it is with Your own
Heart that I glorify God, our Father, as no soul
has ever glorified Him before (*Diary*, 836).

The Silent Heart Of Jesus

Although the desert is fearful, I walk with lifted head and eyes fixed on the sun; that is to say, on the merciful Heart of Jesus (*Diary*, 886).

† In difficult moments, I will fix my gaze upon the silent Heart of Jesus, stretched upon the Cross, and from the exploding flames of His merciful Heart, will flow down upon me power and strength to keep fighting (*Diary*, 906).

† When great sufferings will cause my nature to tremble, and my physical and spiritual strength will diminish, then will I hide myself deep in the open wound of the Heart of Jesus, silent as a dove, without complaint (*Diary* 957).

O Treasure Of My Heart

I snuggled close to Jesus' Heart, because
I realized that I had been thinking too
much about creatures (*Diary,* 960).

"My heart wants nothing but You alone,
O Treasure of my heart. For all the gifts
You give me, thank You, O Lord, but I
desire only Your Heart" (*Diary,* 969).

When I see that the burden is beyond
my strength, I do not consider or analyze
it or probe into it, but I run like a child to
the Heart of Jesus and say only one word
to Him: "You can do all things." And then
I keep silent, because I know
that Jesus Himself will intervene
in the matter, and as for me,
instead of tormenting myself,
I use that time to love Him
(*Diary,* 1033).

NESTLING CLOSE TO THE SACRED HEART

At that moment, a ray of light illumined my soul, and I saw the whole abyss of my misery. In that same moment I nestled close to the Most Sacred Heart of Jesus with so much trust that even if I had the sins of all the damned weighing on my conscience, I would not have doubted God's mercy but, with a heart crushed to dust, I would have thrown myself into the abyss of Your mercy (*Diary*, 1318).

I entrust myself to You as a little child does to its mother's love. Even if all things were to conspire against me, and even if the ground were to give way under my feet, I would be at peace close to Your Heart. You are always a most tender mother to me, and You surpass all mothers (*Diary*, 1490).

THE DEPTHS OF HIS MERCY

Most merciful Heart of Jesus, protect us
from the just anger of God (*Diary*, 1526).

With great patience, I will listen when
others open their hearts to me, accept their
sufferings, give them spiritual comfort, but
drown my own sufferings in the most merciful
Heart of Jesus. I will never leave the depths
of His mercy, while bringing the whole
world into those depths (*Diary*, 1550).

*H*IDE ME IN YOUR DEPTHS

O Jesus, it is through Your most compassionate Heart, as through a crystal, that the rays of Divine Mercy have come to us (*Diary*, 1553).

We expect to obtain everything promised us by Jesus in spite of all our wretchedness. For Jesus is our Hope: Through His merciful Heart, as through an open gate, we pass through to heaven (*Diary*, 1570).

† O Wound of Mercy, Heart of Jesus, hide me in Your depths as a drop of Your own Blood, and do not let me out forever! Lock me in Your depths, and do You Yourself teach me to love You! Eternal Love, do You Yourself form my soul that it be made capable of returning Your love (*Diary*, 1631).

Holy Spirit

December 12 - 14

*I*n seeking to be holy, St. Faustina developed a special devotion to the Holy Spirit. She recognized that "faithfulness to the inspirations of the Holy Spirit" is "the shortest route [to holiness]" (*Diary*, 291). She even laments over souls who don't seek the inspiration of the Holy Spirit, "Oh, if souls would only be willing to listen, at least a little, to the voice of conscience and the voice — that is, the inspirations of the Holy Spirit! (*Diary*, 359).

Saint Faustina particularly underscored the value of silence in cultivating the inspiration of the Holy Spirit. "The silent soul is capable of attaining the closest union with God," she wrote. "It lives almost always under the inspiration of the Holy Spirit. God works in a silent soul without hindrance" (*Diary*, 477).

What about us? Do we take time for silence in God's presence as part of our daily prayer life? If we do, do we also ask for the inspiration of the Holy Spirit when our hearts have been stilled? Let's seek His inspiration today!

THE FAINTEST BREATH OF THE HOLY SPIRIT

O Spirit of God, Director of the soul,
wise is he whom You have trained! But
for the Spirit of God to act in the soul,
peace and recollection are needed
(*Diary*, 145).

A noble and delicate soul ... follows
faithfully the faintest breath of the
Holy Spirit; it rejoices in this Spiritual
Guest and holds onto Him like a child
to its mother (*Diary*, 148).

In my interior life I never reason;
I do not analyze the ways in
which God's Spirit leads me.
It is enough for me to know
that I am loved and that I love.
(*Diary*, 293).

THE SILENT SOUL AND THE HOLY SPIRIT

Oh, if souls would only be willing to listen, at least a little, to the voice of conscience and the voice — that is, the inspirations — of the Holy Spirit! I say "at least a little," because once we open ourselves to the influence of the Holy Spirit, He Himself will fulfill what is lacking in us (*Diary*, 359).

The silent soul is capable of attaining the closest union with God. It lives almost always under the inspiration of the Holy Spirit. God works in a silent soul without hindrance (*Diary*, 477).

Virtue without prudence is not virtue at all. We should often pray to the Holy Spirit for this grace of prudence (*Diary*, 1106).

$\mathcal{F}$AITHFUL TO THE SPIRIT'S INSPIRATIONS

My heart has been accustomed to the inspirations of the Holy Spirit, to whom I am faithful. In the midst of the greatest din I have heard the voice of God. I always know what is going on in my interior ... (*Diary*, 1504).

O Jesus, keep me in holy fear, so that I may not waste graces. Help me to be faithful to the inspirations of the Holy Spirit. Grant that my heart may burst for love of You, rather than I should neglect even one act of love for You (*Diary*, 1557).

Saving Souls

December 15 - 24

Saint Faustina describes a very important aspect of her mission of mercy as saving souls. She was willing to suffer and sacrifice — to go to any length — to help Jesus save souls. And in this all-important battle for souls, her weapon was mercy. The great Apostle of Mercy wrote, "I shall fight all evil with the weapon of mercy. I am being burned up by the desire to save souls. I traverse the world's length and breadth and venture as far as its ultimate limits and its wildest lands to save souls. I do this through prayer and sacrifice" (*Diary,* 745).

In praying for the salvation of souls, St. Faustina would enter into the reality of Holy Mass and the Lord's Passion for poor sinners. "Take everything away from me, but give me souls," she told the Lord Jesus. "I want to become a sacrificial host for sinners. Let the shell of my body conceal my offering, for Your Most Sacred Heart is also hidden in a Host, and certainly You are a living sacrifice" (*Diary,* 908).

We, too, should offer our prayers, sufferings, and sacrifices for the salvation of souls — uniting them to Jesus' sacrifice on the Cross. Let's make a point of doing just that, especially whenever we participate in the Holy Sacrifice of the Mass. As we do, let's remember in particular our own family members, friends, and neighbors whose souls may be in peril.

THE WORK OF SAVING IMMORTAL SOULS

I desire to struggle, toil, and empty myself
for our work of saving immortal souls
(*Diary*, 194).

I will do everything within my power to
save souls, and I will do it through prayer
and suffering (*Diary*, 735).

O Savior of the world. I unite myself with
Your mercy. My Jesus, I join all my sufferings
to Yours and deposit them in the treasury
of the Church for the benefit of souls
(*Diary*, 740).

Burned Up By The Desire To Save Souls

† I shall fight all evil with the weapon of mercy. I am being burned up by the desire to save souls. I traverse the world's length and breadth and venture as far as its ultimate limits and its wildest lands to save souls. I do this through prayer and sacrifice (*Diary*, 745).

I will praise God for His infinite goodness, and I will strive to bring other souls to know and glorify the inexpressible and incomprehensible mercy of God (*Diary*, 753).

THE RAYS OF MERCY SAVE SOULS

Jesus, my spirit yearns for You, and I desire very much to be united with You, but Your works hold me back. The number of souls that I am to bring to You is not yet complete (*Diary*, 761).

I take into my hands the two rays that spring from Your merciful Heart; that is, the Blood and the Water; and I scatter them all over the globe so that each soul may receive Your mercy and, having received it, may glorify it for endless ages (*Diary*, 836).

$\mathcal{A}$ Great Multitude Of Souls

O human souls, where are you going to
hide on the day of God's anger: Take refuge
now in the fount of God's mercy. O what a
great multitude of souls I see! They worshiped
The Divine Mercy and will be singing the
hymn of praise for all eternity (*Diary*, 848).

There are times in life when the soul finds
comfort only in profound prayer. Would that
souls knew how to persevere in prayer at
such times. This is very important (*Diary*, 860).

*L*ET YOUR MERCY
REST UPON SINNERS

Taking advantage of the intimacy to which the Lord was admitting me, I interceded before Him for the whole world. At such moments I have the feeling that the whole world is depending on me (*Diary*, 870).

Jesus, give me the souls of sinners; let Your mercy rest upon them. Take everything away from me, but give me souls. I want to become a sacrificial host for sinners (*Diary*, 908).

I Live For Souls

I often accompany a person who is dying far away, but my greatest joy is when I see the promise of mercy fulfilled in these souls (*Diary*, 935).

I am constantly united with [the Lord], and I am fully aware that I live for souls in order to bring them to Your mercy, O Lord. In this matter, no sacrifice is too insignificant (*Diary*, 971).

Begging God's Mercy For Every Soul

I feel that I am being completely transformed into prayer in order to beg God's mercy for every soul. O my Jesus, I am receiving You into my heart as a pledge of mercy for souls (*Diary*, 996).

I suffer great pain at the sight of the sufferings of others. All these sufferings are reflected in my heart. I carry their torments in my heart so that it even wears me out physically. I would like all pains to fall upon me so as to bring relief to my neighbor (*Diary*, 1039).

*H*OW MANY SOULS ARE CALLING OUT

My Jesus, penetrate me through and through so that I might be able to reflect You in my whole life. Divinize me so that my deeds may have supernatural value. Grant that I may have love, compassion, and mercy for every soul without exception (*Diary*, 1242).

The Lord gave me to know how much He desires a soul to distinguish itself by deeds of love. And in spirit I saw how many souls are calling out to us, "Give us God." And the blood of the Apostles boiled up within me. I will not be stingy with it; I will shed it all to the last drop for immortal souls (*Diary*, 1249).

I Want The Salvation Of Souls

† Christ, give me souls. Let anything You like
happen to me, but give me souls in return. I want
the salvation of souls. I want souls to know Your
mercy. I have nothing left for myself, because I
have given everything away to souls, with the result
that on the day of judgment I will stand before
You empty-handed, since I have given everything
away to souls. Thus You will have nothing on
which to judge me, and we shall meet on
that day: Love and mercy (*Diary,* 1426).

† I make constant efforts in practicing virtue.
I try faithfully to follow Jesus. And I deposit
this whole series of daily virtues — silent, hidden,
almost imperceptible, but made with great love
— in the treasury of God's Church for the
common benefit of souls. I feel interiorly as
if I were responsible for all souls
(*Diary,* 1505).

RESPONSIBLE FOR ALL SOULS

† I feel interiorly as if I were responsible for
all souls. I know very well that I do not live
for myself alone, but for the entire Church ...
(*Diary*, 1505).

What I talk to You about, Jesus, is our secret,
which creatures shall not know and Angels dare
not ask about. These are secret acts of forgiveness,
known only to Jesus and me; this is the mystery
of His mercy, which embraces each soul separately
(*Diary*, 1692).

Humility, Humiliation

December 25 - 31

Saint Faustina learned that humility is the bedrock foundation of the spiritual life. Repeatedly, she was told of the importance of humility by the Lord, Our Blessed Mother, and her confessor, Fr. Joseph Andrasz, SJ. Jesus told her, **"My daughter, let three virtues adorn you in a particular way: humility, purity of intention, and love"** (*Diary*, 1779).

Out of love for the Lord, St. Faustina also faced many humiliations through serious illness and even persecution at the hands of her fellow religious sisters. She would even thank the Lord for these sorts of humiliations, saying, "I thank the Lord for every humiliation and will pray specially for the person who has given me the chance to be humiliated" (*Diary*, 243).

To grow in humility, St. Faustina looked especially to the example of Jesus, the humble Savior. She advised, "He who wants to learn true humility should reflect upon the Passion of Jesus" (*Diary*, 267).

Humility was characteristic of both Jesus and Mary, and they demanded humility of St. Faustina. So, the gems on humility begin on Christmas Day when Jesus, the Son of God, humbled Himself to become man, born of Mary. He is truly Emmanuel, God-with-us! And He calls us to be humble.

THE IMMORTAL KING

How can this be; You are God and I —
I am Your creature. You, the Immortal King
and I, a beggar and misery itself! But now all
is clear to me; Your grace and Your love, O Lord,
will fill the gulf between You, Jesus, and me
(*Diary*, 199).

† I will thank the Lord Jesus for every
humiliation and will pray specially for the
person who has given me the chance to
be humiliated (*Diary*, 243).

Reflect Upon The Passion Of Jesus

He who wants to learn true humility should reflect upon the Passion of Jesus (*Diary*, 267).

Satan defeats only the proud and the cowardly, because the humble are strong. Nothing will confuse or frighten a humble soul (*Diary*, 450).

O Jesus, my heart stops beating when I think of all You are doing for me! I am amazed at You, Lord, that You would stoop so low to my wretched soul! What inconceivable means You take to convince me! (*Diary*, 460).

A Truly Happy Soul Is Humble

I will not offer explanations on my own behalf
or seek to vindicate myself when criticized;
I will let others judge me as they will (*Diary*, 504).

O my Jesus, nothing is better for the soul than
humiliations. In contempt is the secret of happiness,
when the soul recognizes that, of itself, it is only
wretchedness and nothingness, and that whatever
it possesses of good is a gift of God (*Diary*, 593).

If there is a truly happy soul upon earth, it
can only be a truly humble soul (*Diary*, 593).

God Defends The Humble Soul

A humble soul does not trust itself, but places
all its confidence in God. (*Diary*, 593).

God defends the humble soul and lets Himself
into its secrets, and the soul abides in
unsurpassable happiness which no one
can comprehend (*Diary*, 593).

THE DEPTH OF JESUS' MEEKNESS AND HUMILITY

Jesus gave me to know the depth of His meekness and humility and to understand that He clearly demanded the same of me (*Diary*, 758).

The Lord, so very great though He is, delights in humble souls. The more a soul humbles itself, the greater the kindness with which the Lord approaches it (*Diary*, 1092).

O Humility, Lovely Flower

Grace from God was given to me precisely
because I was the weakest of all people; this
is why the Almighty has surrounded me
with His special mercy (*Diary,* 1099).

O humility, lovely flower, I see how few
souls possess you. Is it because you are so beautiful
and at the same time so difficult to attain? O yes,
it is both the one and the other. Even God takes
great pleasure in her (*Diary,* 1306).

† Now I understand why there are so few saints;
it is because so few souls are deeply humble
(*Diary,* 1306).

A LOWLY AND DEEPLY HUMBLE SOUL

O Lord, You who penetrate my whole being and the most secret depths of my soul, You see that I desire You alone and long only for the fulfillment of Your holy will, paying no heed to difficulties or sufferings or humiliations or to what others might think (*Diary*, 1360).

Lord, although You often make known to me the thunders of Your anger, Your anger vanishes before lowly souls. Although You are great, Lord, You allow yourself to be overcome by a lowly and deeply humble soul (*Diary*, 1436).